BORN TO FLY

THE FIRST WOMEN'S AIR RACE ACROSS AMERICA

ALSO BY STEVE SHEINKIN

★

Undefeated:
Jim Thorpe and the Carlisle Indian School Football Team

Most Dangerous:
Daniel Ellsberg and the Secret History of the Vietnam War

The Port Chicago 50:
Disaster, Mutiny, and the Fight for Civil Rights

Bomb:
The Race to Build—and Steal—the World's Most Dangerous Weapon

The Notorious Benedict Arnold:
A True Story of Adventure, Heroism & Treachery

Which Way to the Wild West?:
Everything Your Schoolbooks Didn't Tell You About Westward Expansion

Two Miserable Presidents:
Everything Your Schoolbooks Didn't Tell You About the Civil War

King George: What Was His Problem?:
Everything Your Schoolbooks Didn't Tell You About the American Revolution

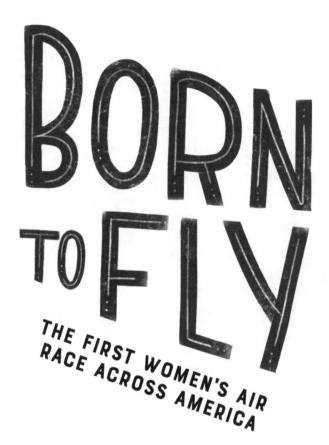

BORN TO FLY

THE FIRST WOMEN'S AIR RACE ACROSS AMERICA

STEVE SHEINKIN

ILLUSTRATIONS BY **BIJOU KARMAN**

ROARING BROOK PRESS ▧ *NEW YORK*

Text copyright © 2019 by Steve Sheinkin
Illustrations copyright © 2019 by Bijou Karman
Published by Roaring Brook Press
Roaring Brook Press is a division of Holtzbrinck Publishing Holdings Limited Partnership
120 Broadway, New York, NY 10271
mackids.com

Library of Congress Cataloging-in-Publication Data

Names: Sheinkin, Steve, author. | Karman, Bijou, illustrator.
Title: Born to fly : the first women's air race across America / Steve Sheinkin ;
    illustrations by Bijou Karman.
Description: First edition. | New York : Roaring Brook Press, [2019] | Audience: 10–14. |
    Includes bibliographical references and index.
Identifiers: LCCN 2018051788 | ISBN 9781626721302 (hardcover)
Subjects: LCSH: Powder Puff Derby—Juvenile literature. | Women air pilots—United States—
    History—Juvenile literature. | Airplane racing—United States—History—Juvenile literature.
Classification: LCC GV759.2.P74 S54 2019 | DDC 797.5/2—dc23
LC record available at https://lccn.loc.gov/2018051788

Our books may be purchased in bulk for promotional, educational, or business use. Please contact
your local bookseller or the Macmillan Corporate and Premium Sales Department at (800) 221-7945
ext. 5442 or by email at MacmillanSpecialMarkets@macmillan.com.

First edition, 2019
Book design by Cassie Gonzales
Printed in the United States of America by LSC Communications, Harrisonburg, Virginia

10 9 8 7 6 5 4 3 2 1

For my daughter, Anna, and my son, David

CONTENTS

BORN TO FLY

They were the kinds of kids who jumped off the roofs of buildings.

Louise McPhetridge did it when she was just seven—climbed to the roof of her family's barn in Bentonville, Arkansas, opened a giant umbrella, and leapt. Not the best idea, maybe, but she *did* aim for a haystack, and wasn't badly hurt.

And besides, she had a perfectly good reason. She *knew* she was born to fly.

Ruth Elder balanced on top of a shed in Anniston, Alabama. She was about twelve. She called to her pony. It came charging. Anxious girls and boys gazed up as Ruth bent her knees, waited, waited—and sprang from the shed, landing with a smack on the back of the galloping horse.

Marvel Crosson was thirteen when she attempted her first flight. She and her younger brother, Joe, had been walking home from school that day in Sterling, Colorado, when they noticed people streaming into the county fairgrounds. Marvel and Joe had no money to get in. They found a hole in the fairground fence and peeked through.

There on the grass, right in front of their eyes, was a flying machine. Or was it?

This was 1913, just ten years after the Wright brothers made the world's first powered flight. Airplanes were still very much a work in progress. Most Americans had never even seen one. The thing on the field looked like a chair with flimsy fly's wings. Behind the seat was a chugging motor and a giant fan.

A man sat in the seat. He shouted something. The motor roared louder. The fan blades spun. The rickety contraption bounced down the field, gaining speed, and then, somehow, *incredibly*, defied gravity and lifted into the air. Marvel had to remind herself to breathe.

As the plane flew low buzzing circles over the crowd, Joe, who was ten, started jumping up and down and hollering, "I'm going to be an aviator! I'm going to be an aviator!"

With its propeller behind the pilot's seat, this early aircraft design was called a "pusher." And yes, it actually took off.

Marvel didn't shout or jump. She didn't say a word. She just quietly made a decision—flying was the only thing she would ever want to do.

Starting now.

Back at the family home, she grabbed an umbrella—not quite wings, but the closest thing she could find—and she and Joe scrambled to the roof of the garage. She opened the umbrella and inched to the edge of the roof and was about to take off when her mother sprinted out of the house, yelping and waving her arms.

The flight was canceled. Or, to be more precise, postponed.

Amelia Earhart didn't jump off a roof. Not exactly.

When she was about eight, she realized the top of the shed in the yard of her family's Kansas City, Kansas, home was the perfect starting spot for a roller coaster. She and her sister, Muriel—Amelia called her Pidge—hammered two-by-fours into tracks and leaned the ride against the roof. They greased the tracks with lard from the icebox and found a wooden crate to use as a car.

Amelia insisted on going first. She carried the crate to the roof and crammed herself in, knees against chest. Pidge and their friend Ralphie stood on the top rung of a ladder, holding the car in place.

"Let me go!"

The crate shot forward, much faster than expected. The track broke with a thunderous *crack*, catapulting car and rider into the air. Amelia soared across the yard, slammed into the grass, and tumbled to a stop.

Alarmed adults ran out from nearby houses.

Amelia leaped up, her dress torn, bleeding from her lip, eyes flaming with joy.

"Oh Pidge," she shouted, "it's just like flying!"

Amelia Earhart may as well have been speaking for all the pilots in this story. The goal was always to get in the air.

After thousands of years of gazing with envy at birds in the sky, humans could suddenly climb into a plane and fly. This is a story about young women who wanted in on the action. They were in a hurry to know how planes worked and to learn how to fly them. They were eager to test themselves against each other, to push planes faster and higher, to smash each other's records in the sky. These are the pilots who would compete in the spectacular Women's Air Derby of 1929, the first women's cross-country air race—and the most controversial air race the country had ever seen.

Air racing was among America's most popular sports in the 1920s, and cross-country races were the Super Bowls of their time. Aviation was new and incredibly dangerous, so when daring pilots set out to race unreliable planes over mountains and across deserts, it made for thrilling drama. These multi-day races featured fierce rivalries, back-and-forth battles for the lead, violent storms, and mechanical failures in the air. There were *always* crashes in these races. In almost every race, at least one pilot was killed.

The first Women's Air Derby would be no exception.

The twenty pilots who would meet in the derby came from all over the country, each with her own story. But they had a lot in common. Besides jumping off roofs.

All were born in the last few years of the nineteenth century or the first few years of the twentieth. They were girls who loved tools and mechanical things, rough sports and risky adventures. They were the kinds of kids who got called "daredevils" and "tomboys." Ruth Elder was typical of the group. She didn't mind being different. She *did* mind that her school wouldn't let her try out for football.

When Marvel Crosson's parents spent their life savings on a new automobile, Marvel took the entire engine apart. She wanted to figure out how it worked—and make it go faster. Mr. Crosson walked into the garage and was horrified to find his children, Marvel and Joe, sitting on the floor surrounded by tiny pieces of his prized possession. The kids put the car back together. It wasn't any faster, but it ran.

At age eleven, four years after her umbrella flight, Louise McPhetridge upgraded to a hot-air balloon. She and some boys from the neighborhood cut canvas from a porch awning, tied it with ropes into the shape of a big balloon, and heated the air inside with oil lamps.

It was time to fly. The boys were nervous.

"It's not so awful big," a kid named Richard said of their invention. "We better let Lou go up."

Lou wouldn't have it any other way. She climbed onto the roof of a shed with the entire contraption strapped to her back and was all set for a test flight when Richard's mother looked out an upstairs window of her house and saw a girl with an oddly bloated backpack about to leap into the sky.

It was another canceled flight.

The winter after her roller-coaster experiment, Amelia Earhart got a new sled. And a stern warning: The correct way for girls to ride a sled was sitting up. Lying on your belly was faster, but not ladylike.

Amelia promptly climbed a steep and icy street, dropped belly-down onto her sled, and pushed off.

She was flying down the hill when a horse pulling a loaded cart stepped out from a side street and stood directly in her path. There was no time to turn, barely time to scream, before the sled sped *between* the horse's front and back legs, *under* its massive belly, and on down the street.

Lucky she hadn't been sitting up like a good girl. To Amelia, that was the lesson.

Her grandmother took a different view. "You don't realize," she lectured, "that when I was a small girl, I did nothing more strenuous than roll my hoop in the public square."

Amelia made an effort. For a few days, she walked calmly through her grandmother's front gate, instead of jumping over the fence.

Too boring. She went back to jumping.

As she'd later explain, "Some elders have to be shocked for everyone's good now and then."

That's something else these future fliers had in common—they were constantly being told to behave more like "proper girls." They were the kinds of kids who defied the command and went right on being themselves.

At her family's home in Southern California, Florence Lowe, another future derby pilot, rode horses when she was supposed to be inside sipping tea. She tracked mud and manure through the formal living room, then used her frilly dresses to clean her riding boots. At school, she challenged the boys to spitting contests. Horrified, the Lowes shipped their daughter to a series of boarding schools, each stricter than the last, but harsh discipline and stiff uniforms proved no match for Florence. One day she brought her horse, Dobbins, into her dorm room. The principal called her to his office and demanded an explanation.

"Poor Dobbins," she said with a straight face, "he must have been so lonesome that he came upstairs to look for me."

They were kids who fell in love with planes at first sight. They were girls who were told that flying was not for them.

Evelyn Trout's first vision of flight was similar to Marvel's. Evelyn—known to friends as Bobbi—was twelve, walking home from school in Hamilton, Canada, where she was staying with relatives. She heard the sound of an engine. An engine in the sky. The grinding noise got louder and louder. She looked up, shading her eyes with her hand, and there it was.

"An airplane!"

She watched, frozen in place, until the plane slipped over the trees and out of sight. Bobbi sprinted home. She had to tell *someone*. She found her aunt Edna in the basement, arms full of jars of preserved vegetables.

"I loved school," Amelia Earhart recalled, "though I never qualified as teacher's pet."

Marvel Crosson—looking ready to leap.

Bobbi Trout (second from left) with high school friends.

Florence Lowe, teen rebel.

Never one to take it slow, Louise McPhetridge left home for college at sixteen.

"Someday I'll be up there!" Bobbi whooped. "Someday I'm going to fly an airplane!"

Aunt Edna smiled at her niece. The kid had always marched to her own drummer. At five years old, she'd announced she was done with dolls and wanted tools instead for Christmas. But flying airplanes? That was taking it too far.

Edna said, "Young ladies of good families do not fly airplanes."

All the pilots in this story heard some version of that lecture.

These girls grew up at a time when life for women in the United States was very different from today. Until 1920, when the pilots were kids or teens, women in most states were not even allowed to *vote*. That finally changed with the ratification of the Nineteenth Amendment to the Constitution—but opportunities for American women were still severely limited.

In high school, Amelia Earhart started collecting articles about women working in fields she found interesting: medicine, law, engineering, film. These jobs were so completely dominated by men, the few women who broke into them made the news. As Amelia knew, women who wanted careers were expected to stick to traditionally female fields: teaching, nursing, social work. Important work, but what if that wasn't what you wanted to do? What if your heart was set on the cutting-edge world of aviation?

The generations of women who had fought for and won the right to vote had faced resentment, angry opposition, even the threat of physical harm. This harsh and very recent history was painfully clear to the pioneering pilots of the Women's Air Derby.

"In those days," Marvel Crosson later explained, "flying was regarded as dangerous for men and impossible for women."

RACING TO THE SKY

Marvel. That was her real name.

Her mother, Elizabeth Crosson, had read a novel called *Marvel* while pregnant and liked the sound of the name. And maybe she knew, when she first saw her baby girl, that the kid would live up to it.

An athletic teen, with bright eyes and curly black hair, Marvel devoured every book and article she could find on aviation. She talked endlessly about flying, about getting her own plane one day. But she'd never actually been on a flight.

In the summer of 1919, after she graduated high school, Marvel and her family set off on a road trip to California. In San Diego, she and Joe dropped their parents off at yet another historical site, then slipped away to *their* idea of a tourist attraction—Dutch Flats airfield.

It was a glimpse of heaven.

"There were planes everywhere!" Marvel remembered. "Pilots going about their business just as though it was the most natural thing in the world."

A pilot walked up and offered them a ride for five dollars each.

"We've only got two-fifty," Marvel said.

They were in luck. Business was slow.

"Hop in," the man said. "Both of you."

It was a little, open-cockpit plane with two seats, one behind the other. The pilot jumped into the back seat. Marvel and Joe put on borrowed goggles and crammed into the front. The pilot gunned the engine, darted down the grass airstrip, and rose into the air so quickly Marvel's chin slammed into her chest.

Marvel, like so many of the pilots in this story, would later *try* to describe the thrill of her first flight, the full-body sensation of soaring in an open cockpit, the pure freedom of it, the blast of air in her face, the views of earth from above, the music of the vibrating metal wires between the wings.

The plane circled one thousand feet above the field for ten minutes. To Marvel, it was ten seconds.

Back on the ground, Marvel and Joe walked in a daze to the car. They sat a long while in silence.

Finally, Joe turned to his sister and said what she'd already been thinking.

"Marvel, that settles it. We've got to have a plane!"

There were some practical problems with the plan. First, planes were expensive. She and Joe had no money. That was solvable. They'd get jobs and save. It would just take time.

Also, the family lived in rural Colorado. There were no airfields nearby. Nowhere to take flying lessons. The solution, they decided, was to persuade their parents to move with them to sunny San Diego. All the way home, and for a solid year after, they gave their parents what Marvel called "the California treatment." It eventually worked.

Marvel got a job in a camera store in San Diego. Joe found work as a car mechanic. They saved every penny. One day, when Marvel was getting ready to leave for work, Joe came rushing in. He had big news but wouldn't say what it was, only that she had to take the afternoon off and come with him.

He explained as they sped across town—a customer at his garage had been talking about flying. He said he'd heard of an airplane for sale, a little navy trainer left over from World War I. The guy who'd owned it had died in a crash. In a different plane, that is.

Joe parked at a waterfront warehouse, and they jumped out. The man at the garage had been right. There was an airplane. Sort of. Technically, there was a stack of wooden crates with airplane parts packed inside.

After a bit of bargaining, the owner's widow agreed to sell for $150—a little over $2,000 in today's money. Together, Marvel and Joe had just enough. They wedged the crates into their car, raced home, hauled everything to the yard behind their house, and started to put their airplane together.

"When Mother and Father saw what we had done, there was quite a revolution," Marvel later recalled. "In addition to messing up the backyard, they were sure that we both were planning to get killed."

By this point, though, the Crosson parents had abandoned hope that their children would lose interest in flying. Marvel knew everything would be okay when she overheard her dad say to her mom, "Well, if anything is going to happen to those kids, it'll happen anyhow. Let them alone—they're happy!"

About 120 miles to the north, on a hot afternoon in 1920, Amelia Earhart and her father, Edwin, walked across the grass of Kinner Field in Los Angeles.

Earhart was twenty-three, tall and thin, her long brown hair in two neat braids. She'd started college a few years before, but then, moved by the sight of wounded soldiers returning from the First World War, had left school to work as a nurse's aide in a veterans hospital. She met pilots and, for the first time, took an interest in aviation. One particular flight changed the course of her life. She was at a fair with a friend. A flier was doing stunts in the sky, sunlight bouncing off the plane's red wings as it twisted and rolled. The plane climbed high, hung for a moment in the air, then nosed down into a screaming dive—directly toward Amelia and her friend.

The friend bolted. Amelia stood still.

She would later describe a rush of fear and pleasure as the plane dove at her. If the pilot lost control even for a second, they'd both die in a ball of flames.

The pilot pulled out of the dive and zipped just feet above Amelia's head.

"I did not understand it at the time," she'd later say, "but I believe that little red airplane said something to me as it swished by."

Now Amelia Earhart was living with her family in Los Angeles, trying to figure out what to do with her life. She had no thought of cross-country races or world fame. She just wanted to learn to fly. She'd heard there was a woman at Kinner Field who gave flying lessons, and she was hoping to sign up.

And there on the field, stepping out of her plane, was the woman she'd come to see, Neta Snook. Snook pulled off her goggles and flying helmet. She shook out her curly red hair and leaned on the wing of her plane.

It would have to be a short rest. Snook took passengers up for rides, and her mechanic was already prepping the next customer.

"Do *not* touch the controls, and do *not* put your feet on the rudder bar," the mechanic told a nervous-looking man. "Do you understand?"

"Yes," the man said. "Will you please tell her not to go too high? I've never been up before, much less with a woman driver."

Typical. As one of the only female pilots in the entire country, Snook had heard it all before.

She was strapping her helmet back on when Amelia Earhart walked up, her father a pace behind.

"I see you are busy," Amelia said, "but could I have a few words with you?"

"Yes, of course," Snook said.

"I want to fly. Will you teach me?"

Snook liked this person. She seemed confident. Got right to the point. They agreed to start lessons the next morning. While they talked over the details, Amelia ran her hand gently along the wings of the plane.

Edwin Earhart appeared less enthused. Amelia smiled at him.

"My parents," she told Snook, "aren't in accord with my ambitions."

That was another thing these women had in common: nervous parents. To be fair, there was reason to worry. The story of early aviation is a story of trial and error.

Error, in this context, means crashing.

In 1908, five years after making the world's first powered flight, Orville and Wilbur Wright traveled to France to demonstrate their flying machine. A young woman named Raymonde de Laroche was amazed by the Wright brothers' invention and decided to become the first female pilot. On a training flight, while coming in for a landing, the tail of her plane clipped a tree, and she hit the ground hard, breaking her collarbone and knocking her unconscious.

It wasn't the injuries that bothered her, though—it was the fear that some other woman would beat her into the air. Rushing her recovery, she was back to her lessons two months later. In March 1910, Raymonde de Laroche became the first woman to earn a pilot's license.

A small handful of daring American women jumped into aviation and, from the very start, raced one another to test limits in the sky. Harriet Quimby, the first American woman to get her license, flew her flimsy craft over the English Channel from England to France in the spring of 1912. The death-defying flight over twenty-six miles of open water would have been major news—but newspapers were filled with stories of a ship called *Titanic*, which had sunk the day before.

Matilde Moisant, who earned her license two weeks after Quimby, pushed

"It is to the air that I have dedicated myself," said Raymonde de Laroche, "and I always fly without the slightest fear."

As soon as she saw hot air balloons at a county fair as a young girl, Neta Snook knew she had to fly.

Blanche Stuart Scott was the first woman to drive a car across the United States—and one of the first to take to the air.

Matilde Moisant described flying as "so wonderful, so exhilarating, so different from everything else in the world."

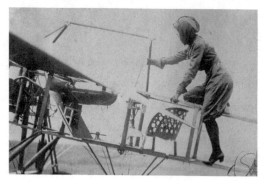

When she wasn't flying, Harriet Quimby kept busy writing magazine articles and movies.

her plane to a women's altitude record of 2,500 feet. Blanche Stuart Scott stunned air show crowds with her famous "Death Dive," in which she'd climb high and dive straight toward earth, pulling out of the fall just one hundred feet from the ground. It didn't always work. Scott had her share of crack-ups and was known to boast of her forty-one mended bones.

That was just part of the deal, the price pilots paid for defying the laws of gravity. Early airplanes were simply not reliable. In the year 1910 alone, thirty-seven pilots, all men, died in air show accidents in the United States. Newspapers praised them as courageous pioneers who gave their lives to advance a thrilling technology that was clearly going to change the world.

When a woman crashed, it was a whole different story.

In the summer of 1912, at an air show in Boston, Harriet Quimby took a passenger up for a routine ride. High above Boston Harbor, the tail of her plane suddenly jolted upward, probably due to turbulence, and both Quimby and the passenger were ejected from their seats—seat belts were not yet standard equipment in planes. Five thousand fans watched in horror as pilot and passenger fell to their deaths.

Here, newspapers claimed, was proof that women lacked the "coolness" and "judgment" needed for flying. "It would be well," concluded the *New York Times*, "to exclude women from a field of activity in which their presence is unnecessary from any point of view."

Amelia Earhart's father did not agree with this way of thinking. He knew his daughter could handle herself in any situation.

Still, how could a parent help but worry?

"You really weren't serious, were you?" Edwin Earhart asked Amelia after their trip to the airfield. "I thought you were just wishing."

Amelia explained that she was very serious about learning to fly. She would get a job and pay for the lessons herself. There was nothing more to discuss.

Marvel and Joe Crosson spent the warm San Diego nights in their backyard, plane parts and tools spread on the grass, hands and faces smeared with grease. They'd never been happier.

"We gave up everything to the plane," Marvel remembered. "We cut out the movies, dances, and every little thing that would cost money."

The plane they'd bought was a Curtiss N-9, a tiny seaplane used by the navy to train pilots during the First World War. The N-9's cabin was open to the wind and had two seats, one behind the other. It was a biplane—it had two wings, one above the other—with a top speed of about seventy-five miles per hour. The whole thing was made of lightweight wood.

Seriously, wood.

Yes, early plane designers realized that, theoretically, metal had certain advantages. It wouldn't crack and splinter, or get eaten by termites, or catch fire. But they hadn't figured out how to make metal-skinned planes that were affordable *and* light enough to fly *and* strong enough to stay together. In the 1920s, 95 percent of all airplanes were made of wood.

Marvel and Joe assembled their plane, piece by piece. The wings were made of wooden frames that had to be covered with tightly stretched fabric. To help with this step, Marvel and Joe's dad removed the kitchen windows. They passed the wings into the house, and their mom sat at the table, sewing the fabric into place.

Spare moments were spent at the airfield, asking advice and scavenging parts. The plane had come with a large pontoon that fit under the cabin, allowing it to land on water. The siblings found wheels to replace the pontoon. In three months, they were done.

"We were proud of it," Marvel said. "There was nothing the matter with it, except that it had no motor."

Louise McPhetridge finally got airborne when she was fifteen. After mixed success with umbrellas and balloons, she was thrilled when a pilot landed in Bentonville and offered airplane rides, five minutes for five bucks. Louise held out her money with a trembling hand.

"Never mind, sister," the pilot said, thinking she was scared, "you don't have to go if you don't want to."

"Let me get in," she said.

She got in. They flew. She was hooked for life.

Tall and wiry, with a playful smile and short, springy hair, Louise left home for the University of Arkansas in the fall of 1922, earning money for school with a summer job at the J. H. Turner Coal Company in Wichita, Kansas. To Louise, the real draw of Wichita wasn't selling coal—it was the Travel Air Manufacturing Company. She spent all her free time at Travel Air, looking over mechanics' shoulders as they built new planes, watching test flights, going up with the pilots when she could talk her way into it.

One day, when she heard the Travel Air engineers were about to test a new design, she couldn't resist—she slipped out of the office and drove to the airfield. She might have gotten away with it, but Mr. Turner wanted to see the flight, too. He was quite surprised to see his young employee at the field in the middle of her shift.

The next morning, he called her into his office.

"The J. H. Turner Coal Company has no room for salesmen who spend working hours at the airport," he lectured.

She was sure she was about to be fired. Instead, he asked a few questions about her interest in aviation, then sent her back to work.

A few days later, Walter Beech, the owner of Travel Air, called Louise. He'd seen her around his airfield, he said, and his friend Turner spoke highly of her. He had an offer she might find interesting.

She drove right to Beech's apartment. He introduced her to a man named D. C. Warren, explaining that he'd hired Warren to open a Travel Air sales office on the West Coast. Then came the shocker.

"How'd you like to go to California with Mr. Warren and learn the airplane business, Louise?"

Stunned silence. Louise looked back and forth from one man to the other. Was this really happening?

True, the economy was booming. The stock market was going up and up, with no end in sight. Lots of people had money to spend, and it made sense that Travel Air was expanding. But was Walter Beech actually offering her a job? A job in aviation?

He assured her that he was.

Louise sped to her parents' home. She burst through the door, shouting: "I'm going to California! I'm going to learn to fly!"

"Why, that's wonderful!" her younger sister, Alice, cried.

Her mother finally managed, "Oh, Louise . . ."

The family sat at the kitchen table, and Louise told them the whole story. Roy McPhetridge took the news hard, almost as if his daughter had just announced she'd been sentenced to death. Roy and Louise were especially close. He'd always wanted a boy and had been thrilled to discover his girl's love of tools and sports. He taught her to drive a car when she was nine. They called each other "Pal."

But flying airplanes—that was a parent's nightmare.

He seemed near tears as he said, "I'm going to talk to this Beech and Warren . . ."

Louise felt sorry for her dad; she really did. But her mind was made up.

Bobbi Trout sat at the kitchen table of her family's home in Los Angeles, flipping through a newspaper. Now fifteen, she hadn't forgotten being told that "young ladies of good families do not fly airplanes." But that wasn't what had her steamed at the moment.

It was her high school's ridiculous rules. All she wanted to do was take shop class, and they were forcing her to study cooking and sewing with the other girls.

"Boy, did that ruin my feelings," she'd later say. "That broke my heart."

Bobbi turned the page of the newspaper. She stopped at an article about two women who ran a gas station.

"I could do that!" she shouted.

Her father read over her shoulder. He rumpled her short black hair. He knew his daughter and didn't want to change her.

"I bet you could, Bobbi," he said.

The Trout family soon opened the Radio Service Station, so named because the station had an actual radio, a rare thing in the early 1920s—customers came just to listen to the evening programs. Bobbi pumped gas, checked oil, and learned to fix cars. Male drivers seemed surprised by the sight of a teenage girl in mechanic's overalls, and they often felt the need to explain to her how things worked.

"Stop!" cried one driver as Bobbi bent to inflate his tires. "You have to let the old air out before you put in the new air, or the tire will explode!"

No, she politely replied, that was not how tires worked.

Another time, while pumping gas for a customer, Bobbi mentioned her dream of learning to fly. The man told her about a local airfield that offered lessons for $250. As soon as she had the money saved, Bobbi drove her maroon roadster—an open-top, two-seat automobile—to the field, parking outside the air school's office.

She took a moment to drink in the delicious smells of dust and gasoline and oily engine parts. Then she walked in.

GOLDEN AGE

"You may not live to a ripe old age if you disregard any of my instructions, even for a moment."

That was Burdett Fuller's first lesson for Bobbi Trout. A former navy flier who now ran an aviation school, Fuller wanted his students to go into flight lessons with eyes wide open.

Notebook and pencil in hand, Bobbi assured him she was eager to learn.

They walked out to the field, and Burdett showed Bobbi the little plane she'd be learning on, a Curtiss JN-4. The "Jenny," as pilots called this popular model, was a two-seat biplane used as a training plane by the army during World War I and sold off to private owners in the years since.

Bobbi took notes as they walked around the plane, making preflight inspections. Then Burdett told her to climb into the back cockpit and buckle her seat belt—they'd finally become standard in planes. He hopped into the front cockpit.

Bobbi's dream was coming true. She couldn't get the massive grin off her face.

"Pay attention!" Burdett snapped. "This may save your life, and someone else's."

There were sets of controls in both cockpits, and Burdett demonstrated by putting his left hand on the control stick, a wooden stick rising up from the cockpit floor. His right hand went on the throttle, which controlled the amount of fuel flowing into the motor. Feet went on the rudder bar. While controlling the plane with stick and rudder, Burdett lectured, a pilot must check the instruments continually—compass, airspeed, altitude, oil temperature and pressure—while also keeping an eye out for a place to make an emergency landing.

"Okay," he said, "now if I haven't scared you away, let's go flying!"

A mechanic checked to make sure wooden chocks were in place in front of the wheels.

"Switch on!" he called to Burdett.

Burdett flipped on the fuel supply to the motor. "Switch on!"

Now came one of the most dangerous tasks in early aviation—simply

These are the instruments Bobbi Trout would have seen when she climbed into the cockpit of a Curtiss "Jenny."

getting the motor started. With no battery or electric starter, planes were started by manually spinning the propeller. The mechanic reached up and took hold of the propeller blade, set his weight on his heels, and yanked down. The spinning of the propeller got the engine's pistons moving and spark plugs sparking, igniting the fuel. As the motor roared to life, the mechanic purposely fell backward to avoid being sliced by the whirling blades.

Once the chocks were removed from in front of the wheels, Burdett and Bobbi taxied onto the grass field used as a runway. Burdett pushed forward on the throttle, and they rumbled down the field, gaining speed. He pulled back on the stick, and they were in the air.

Bobbi instantly felt it—the dizzying freedom of flight.

Turning in his seat, Burdett saw that his student had lost focus. He reached his hand out of the cockpit and pointed straight down.

Below them was a cemetery.

Bobbi nodded. Message delivered.

Pilots and historians of flight fondly refer to the years between the First and Second World Wars as the "Golden Age" of aviation. Early planes were handcrafted works of engineering and sculpture. With no GPS or autopilot, no control towers to guide them to safe landings, pilots relied on their own nerves and skill. They flew with wind and weather in their faces, using their hands and feet, their brains, and all their senses to move their machines around in the sky.

Flying was done, as pilots liked to say, "by the seat of your pants"—by literally *feeling* through the seat beneath you how the plane was performing, how it was responding to your touch. It took practice and talent, and the only way to find out if you were any good was hands-on, up in the air.

For her early lessons, Amelia Earhart sat in the front of Neta Snook's plane. Snook, piloting from the back, would take the plane up. The roaring engine coughed clouds of hot exhaust into the cockpit. Wind whipped their faces, and waves of turbulence tossed the plane around. Neta would find smooth air, level off, and let Amelia take the controls.

Early airplane controls were simple. Not easy to use, but simple.

Push the stick left, and a hinged flap on the back of the left wing—an aileron—moved up. At the same time, the right aileron angled down. The right wing rose and the left wing dipped, causing plane tilt—"bank," as pilots said—and turn to the left. Pull the stick back, and flaps on the tail—elevators—angled down, forcing the nose of the plane up. Pushing the stick forward moved the nose down, putting the plane into a descent. The rudder pedals controlled the rudder on the tail of the plane, moving the nose of the plane left or right.

At first, Amelia Earhart did what she'd done when she was learning to drive a car—tried too hard, "overcontrolled," as she put it, and the plane wobbled and bobbed. Once she got the feel of flying straight and level, she worked on turning. The trick to a smooth turn, Neta taught her, was to use both stick and rudder, banking the wings and moving the nose at the same time. If the movements were out of balance, the plane would skid sideways, like a car taking a curve too fast.

Snook taught Earhart to constantly watch for places to land. Early motors died. Often. When a car motor failed, you rolled to a stop. It was inconvenient. When a plane motor died in the air, you began to fall from the sky.

New pilots felt safest close to the ground, but you were much better off a few thousand feet up. The added altitude gave you the most valuable resource in a crisis: time. Time to think. Time, hopefully, to glide to a flat field or empty road and put the plane down in one piece.

Amelia was a quick learner, though easily distracted by magnificent views. Which is fine for the passenger. The pilot cannot lose focus. Neta stressed this point again and again.

"I know, I guess I was daydreaming," Amelia told Neta after a typical lapse. "I'll be more careful tomorrow."

Marvel Crosson was still stuck behind the counter of a camera store in San Diego.

When customers came in to drop off film to be developed, she'd ask, "Do you know anyone who wants to sell a good airplane motor?"

They'd look at her like she was crazy.

Her brother had better luck at his job. Joe asked everyone who came into the car-repair shop if they knew where he could buy a plane engine. A customer mentioned he'd heard of a man who was selling a few Curtiss 90-horsepower airplane motors, a perfect fit for the Crossons' plane. Only one catch—the guy insisted the engines be used in boats, not planes. Planes crashed all the time, and he didn't want to be responsible for anyone dying.

Joe and Marvel went to see the man. They told him the motor was for their nice, little boat. How much did he want for it?

He said he'd need to get $125, no less.

They'd expected it to cost $500. Joe, playing it cool, said, "Okay, we'll take one."

They agreed to come back with the money, then drove home, wondering where they were going to get $125. They'd put everything they had into the plane. So they sold their car. They borrowed their father's car to pick up the engine. Neither spoke on the way home, as if frightened of waking from a dream.

That night, unable to sleep, Marvel went out to the backyard to open the box and peek inside.

It took a week to get the engine in. "Joe and I were covered with grease and dirt every evening," Marvel remembered. "Finally, it was in place and the propeller fixed."

The next day, Marvel raced home from work. Joe was already in the yard, waiting.

"Get in the ship, Marvel," Joe said. "I'm going to start her."

She jumped into the cockpit. Joe cranked the propeller. The motor caught. The propeller whirled. Marvel could not resist pulling the throttle wide open, feeding the cylinders the maximum mix of fuel and air, "and the result," she said, "was glorious." The cabin rocked and the motor roared and the propeller spun so fast it disappeared.

Everything worked perfectly—so why was Joe shouting and waving his arms?

Marvel cut the engine. She was about to ask what was wrong when she noticed the feathers. Chicken feathers. It was snowing chicken feathers.

They floated slowly down, landing on Joe, landing on Marvel, settling on the wings of the plane. The blast from the propeller, she realized, had blown them off the neighbor's chickens.

The chickens were fine. Just chilly for a little while.

But would the thing actually fly?

Marvel and Joe had read enough and hung around airfields enough to understand the basic science. Four forces act on planes in flight: drag, weight, thrust, and lift.

Weight is the force of gravity, the force that pulls you down when you jump. A plane like the Crossons' Curtiss N-9 was about two thousand pounds—a lot of weight to get off the ground.

Drag is caused by the friction of an object moving through air. Imagine holding your hand (carefully) out the window of a moving car. The air hits your hand, which slows it down, pushing it back. That's drag.

To overcome drag, a plane uses the force of thrust. Thrust is created by the spinning propeller, which pulls the plane forward.

Creating lift is the job of the wings. As a plane moves forward, the air hitting the front edge of the wing divides, some flowing over the wing and

some under. The slightly curved top of the wing causes air to flow faster over the wing than under it. This creates an area of lower air pressure above the wing than below, and the difference in air pressure creates lift—the wing rises into the area of lower pressure.

Lift may be hard to picture, but for a simple demonstration of the effect of differences in air pressure, get a piece of paper or a dollar bill. Hold one end near your mouth, letting the far end droop down. Blow over the top of the paper and—surprisingly—the far end of the paper will rise. On an airplane, when air flows over a wing fast enough, the lift generated overcomes the force of gravity and the plane takes off.

The physics get complicated, but it always works—assuming the plane is built perfectly.

In the middle of the night, Marvel and Joe towed their homemade craft down empty city streets to Dutch Flats airfield. The next day, they stood and watched as a flight instructor climbed into the cockpit, sped down the grass field—and lifted smoothly into the blue sky.

"It flies! It flies!" Joe hollered. "And it's ours! It's ours!"

Marvel felt like the happiest person on earth.

Now they just needed to learn how to fly.

They didn't have enough money to both take lessons. Joe got his license first, then taught Marvel. She had a natural feel for the controls—though the men at the airfield refused to take her seriously. "Those good fellows never forgot that I was a girl!" she'd later say. "They acted as though it were a pleasant thing for a girl to be interested in flying, but, 'just among us men,' it was of no importance."

Marvel brushed this aside. Joe couldn't. He could see right away his sister had a real talent for flying.

"You're getting good," he told her, "and it won't be long now before we show this gang something they'll not forget in a hurry."

Next time they went up, Joe climbed the plane to one thousand feet.

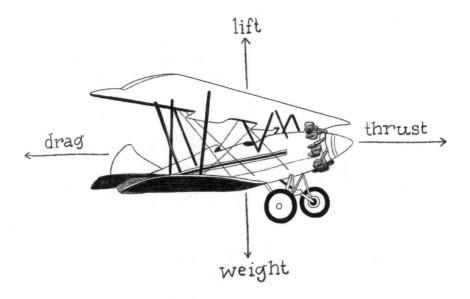

lift

drag

thrust

weight

He let her take the controls and motioned for her to fly over the hangar, where pilots and mechanics were standing around. Marvel banked toward the hangar and watched in shock as Joe climbed out of his seat and stepped onto the plane's lower wing, gripping the brace wires for balance.

Marvel buzzed the hangar with Joe standing on the wing, waving wildly with one hand to a group of astounded aviators.

Soon she was ready for her first solo flight. She went through her preflight checks, including a look at the wind sock on the airfield. The sock, which looked more like a pajama leg on a stick, told her the speed and direction of the wind.

Telling herself it was just another flight, no different from if Joe were with her, Marvel taxied onto the field, swerving in an S pattern to see in front of her—on the ground, a pilot in the cockpit could not see around the front of the plane. She pointed the plane into the wind. Taking off into the wind meant more air flowing over the wings, generating more lift. She zipped forward, took off, circled the field a few times, and brought the plane in for a perfect landing.

Joe rushed up to congratulate her. The entire airport gang was won over. They ran up, clapping and cheering. That night, Joe told their parents the news.

"Marvel," their mother said, grabbing her in a hug, "I'm just as proud as I can be!"

Their dad sat in his chair, quiet. His eyes were wet and twinkling.

The next day, Joe heard him telling friends, "My girl can fly with the best of 'em!"

Florence Lowe took a very different route into the air.

Florence continued her rebellious ways through her teen years. At one of the many boarding schools that tried to tame her, she taped a dagger to her chest, drenched herself in red ink, and sprawled on the floor of her dorm room. When her roommate came in, the poor girl literally tripped over what appeared to be a bloody corpse.

Somehow, Florence graduated from high school. Under relentless family pressure, she agreed to marry the Reverend Rankin Barnes. She tried teaching Sunday school, as was expected of the minister's wife, but wound up shocking the community by giving her nine-year-old pupils pocket knives. She tried learning to cook and clean. She couldn't do it.

"I was no man's maid servant, nor would I ever be!"

Unable to settle down, Florence put on men's clothes, called herself "Jacob Crane," and signed on to the crew of a cargo ship bound for Mexico.

"I think you'll pass as a guy," her friend Roger told her. "Lord knows you've got the temper and language that goes with it."

It was in Mexico, in the spring of 1927, that Florence got her legendary nickname. She and Roger were riding donkeys down a dusty country road, and he joked that she looked like Pancho, sidekick of Don Quixote, the famous fictional knight.

"That wasn't *Pancho*, you numbskull," she snapped, "that was *Sancho!*"

"Pancho, Sancho, who really gives a whoop? I'm going to call you Pancho."

Pancho. Pancho Barnes. That had a ring to it.

Pancho returned to California and her marriage, but she was soon restless again. That's when she remembered the words of her grandfather, Thaddeus Lowe, the one adult who'd ever understood her. A pioneer in the field of hot-air balloons, Lowe had sailed high above Civil War battlefields to gather intelligence for the Union Army. He was a born flier, and he'd seen the same stuff in his granddaughter.

"Everyone will be flying airplanes when you grow up," he once told her. "You'll be a flyer, too."

Pancho Barnes—she liked the sound of that.

A flier—*that's* what she wanted to be.

Pancho found the name of an instructor and drove to the airfield.

"When is it you wanted to start learning?" the man asked, visibly annoyed. He didn't like the idea of teaching women.

"Well," she said, "right now is okay."

Pancho strapped into the front seat. The instructor climbed his plane to one thousand feet and then dove straight down. Pancho watched, helpless, as the earth approached. Her head snapped back as the plane pulled out of the dive and climbed. She hung upside-down as the pilot flew loop after dizzying loop.

Back on the ground, the man turned to her with a wicked grin. "Still want to learn how to fly?"

He'd expected to see her green and quaking. She was glowing with excitement.

"Hell *yes*," Pancho said, "I want to learn to fly!"

DREAMS AND NIGHTMARES

Learning to fly was the easy part. The challenge was learning to survive when things went wrong.

Pancho Barnes got her pilot's license, bought her own plane, and, like all pilots, got into trouble in the air. One evening, she set out for home too late. By the time she was back to her airfield, it was dark. There were no lights on the field. There was no one there to help; Pancho was on her own. She knew approximately where the open grass began and ended, but she couldn't see the ground well enough to be sure of avoiding the trees and power lines she knew were all around.

She circled, running low on fuel, thinking hard. There had to be a solution.

And she got it—the hamburger stand!

There was a hamburger stand, painted white, by the edge of the field. She couldn't see it, but she knew it was there. Circling until the next car drove by on the road below, she watched the car's headlights sweep across the side of the white building. With that as a reference point, Pancho came in for a safe landing.

Marvel Crosson's first close call came high over the Pacific Ocean.

Marvel was reveling in the wonder of flight—the way it cleared her mind and washed away the frustrations of her boring job—when the plane's engine coughed, rattled, and went quiet. The propeller spun to a stop.

The only sound was the whistle of the wind. She was twenty-five miles from shore.

Marvel spotted a navy ship in the distance. Her first thought was to splash down near the ship—if she survived the impact, the sailors could fish her from the water. But she was losing altitude. The ship was too far away. She wasn't going to be able to glide close enough.

Somehow keeping cool, thinking of her reading and training, of all those conversations with pilots, she realized what she had to do.

She shoved the stick forward, putting her plane into a nosedive.

It took icy nerves, trading precious altitude for one shot at restarting the motor. If it didn't work, she'd go down in the water.

The plane accelerated toward the surface of the ocean. The added speed of the air hitting the propeller started the blades spinning, slowly at first, then faster, then whirling, kicking the engine back to life. With water and waves coming up fast at her windshield, Marvel pulled out of the dive, banked, and raced for land.

Amelia Earhart's first crisis did not end as well.

She was at the controls in the back seat with Neta Snook up front. She sped down the grass field and lifted into the air. But the plane didn't climb fast enough—Snook would later blame a clogged cylinder for the sluggish engine. They were flying directly toward the tops of tall trees at the end of the field.

Amelia had a few seconds to choose between two very bad options.

She could push the nose down to gain speed, but that would likely take the plane right into the trees. She could pull back on the stick and try to climb, but the plane wasn't going fast enough to climb.

Earhart pulled back. Snook later said she'd have done the same.

The plane went into a "stall"—one of the main causes of crashes. The motor does not quit in a stall. The motor was running, the propeller was spinning, but air wasn't flowing over the wings fast enough to generate lift. The plane slid down in what felt like sickening slow motion, clearing the trees by sheer luck and slamming into a farmer's field. The propeller broke. The landing gear snapped. The wings collapsed. Amelia was thrust forward and bit her tongue hard enough to draw blood.

But that was the worst of it. Amazingly, she and Neta climbed from the wreckage basically unhurt. A crowd gathered. Someone called the local newspaper, and a reporter showed up.

Amelia Earhart, soon to be one of the most famous people in the world, a hero to millions, gave her first interview in a field of cabbages by the side of a crumpled plane.

Lola Trout found out about her daughter's first crack-up in a Los Angeles newspaper. She turned a page of the evening paper, and a small headline stopped her cold:

GIRL FLYER CRASHES

The article was short on details. A young aviatrix, Evelyn "Bobbi" Trout, had crashed that morning and been rushed to Inglewood Hospital. Lola tossed the paper aside and raced out the door.

She found Bobbi in a hospital bed with a bandage over one eye. Bobbi

had suffered a concussion, a doctor explained, and needed stitches where her flight goggles had sliced into her face. Lola stood by the bed, running her hand over Bobbi's head, as if to assure herself her daughter was really there.

"You might have been killed!" Mrs. Trout wailed.

"Maybe," groaned Bobbi, groggy but conscious. "But in that case, I'd never have known the difference—would I?"

Just what a mother wants to hear.

The next morning, Mrs. Trout brought in a stack of newspapers with articles about the crash, hoping they'd persuade Bobbi to give up flying. The plan backfired. The articles all made it sound like Bobbi had been at the controls, when it had actually been an instructor, Dale Page.

"They never get anything right," Bobbi huffed. "Always blaming the woman."

Airplane and motorcycle—Bobbi Trout's preferred forms of transportation.

She returned to work at the service station with a patch over one eye.

As soon as the patch came off, she was back in the air.

Amelia Earhart's reaction to her first crash was basically the same. She understood that every flight could be her last. And she lived for her next flight.

Earhart spent long, boring weeks in the office of a telephone company, opening mail, filing papers, daydreaming about airplanes. Weekends were for flying.

One Sunday, in long pants and her new leather jacket—practical flying clothes—she rode the city bus toward Kinner Field, got off at the end of the line, and started hiking down a long, dusty road. A car pulled over, and the driver offered her a lift to the field; it was obvious from her outfit where she was headed.

Amelia noticed a young girl in the back seat, staring at her with wonder. As they drove to the field, the girl demanded to know if Earhart was a real-life flier. She said she was.

The girl was thrilled—and puzzled. "But you don't look like an aviatrix," she said. "You have long hair!"

It was true. Long hair was impractical in the air, blowing in the wind, blocking your view. Amelia had been secretly snipping her hair an inch at a time, hoping no one would notice. "It was very odd indeed for a woman to fly," she later explained, "and I had tried to remain as normal as possible in looks in order to offset the usual criticism of my behavior."

It was hopeless. There was no way to do this without criticism.

Amelia Earhart cut her hair short and kept it that way.

Stacking up every dollar of savings, she put a down payment on a plane of her own, a tiny bright-yellow Kinner Airster she named *Canary*, a ship so light she could lift the tail and push it around the field. Soon after her first solo flight, she took her plane up to see how high it could climb. Circling higher and higher above Los Angeles, she pushed the motor until it rattled so violently she thought it might burst from the nose of the plane. When she got back down, she found out she'd reached fourteen thousand feet, higher than any woman had ever flown.

For the second time, Amelia Earhart made the local papers.

Her uncle was not impressed.

"The only time a lady's name should appear in print," he explained to the family, "is at her birth, her marriage, and her funeral."

It was the sort of thing the pilots of the first Women's Air Derby heard a lot.

The United States burst into the 1920s—the Roaring Twenties—as an emerging world power with a booming economy. For the first time in history, more Americans lived in cities than on farms. Families brought home their first radios, telephones, and refrigerators, and people who had grown up with horses and buggies could suddenly afford their own cars. Women had won the right to vote, and a new generation of women now seized a new kind of freedom—the freedom to have *fun*. Nicknamed "flappers," these young women flouted tradition by cutting their hair short, wearing shorter dresses, playing competitive sports, dancing in public to jazz music, even drinking and smoking alongside their male friends.

For some, like Amelia Earhart's stuffy uncle, it was all too much. Too much change happening too fast.

The pilots in this story were hardly flappers; they had no time to follow fashions. At the camera store where she worked, Marvel Crosson stood out for *not* bobbing her hair. When female coworkers asked why she was bucking the trend, Marvel made excuses, knowing they'd never understand the real reason.

"Haircuts cost at least a dollar," she later explained, "and a dollar would buy more than four gallons of fuel for our plane."

In their own way, though, these pilots *were* like flappers. They were rebels, having fun on their own terms. They were weaving through obstacles and chasing their dreams.

Without a doubt, no pilot from this generation overcame greater obstacles than Bessie Coleman. The other pilots were white; Coleman was black. In 1920, a time when racial segregation was an established part of American life, there were no African American pilots in the United States, women or men. Bessie Coleman changed that.

Born in rural Texas in 1892, Coleman moved to Chicago in her early twenties, fell in love with aviation, and went to school after school looking for flying lessons. Not a single one was willing to take her.

"No one had ever heard of a black woman pilot," she recalled. "I refused to take no for an answer."

Bessie sailed to France, found a flying school that would teach her, earned her license, and returned home. She quickly gained fame as a stunt flier at air shows, proving herself to be one of the country's top young fliers. Coleman loved to perform for the crowds, with one exception—she refused to fly at any show that did not allow equal access to African American fans.

Like so many pilots of her time, Bessie Coleman's life was cut short. In 1926, on a test flight with her mechanic in Jacksonville, Florida, the mechanic lost control of the plane, and he and Coleman were killed. She was just thirty-four.

Bessie Coleman's death was front-page news nationwide. It was another reminder of how dangerous aviation was in the 1920s.

Louise McPhetridge's parents did not need another reminder. In the

At air shows and lectures all over the country, Bessie Coleman inspired her audiences to dream big.

spring of 1927, at the Travel Air factory airfield in Wichita, they reluctantly waved good-bye as their daughter climbed into the passenger seat of a plane. Louise's new boss, D. C. Warren, was at the controls. Together they set out for California.

After a four-day trip west, Louise moved into a small apartment in Oakland. Her real home was the airport. She helped run the Travel Air flight school. She worked on the sales floor selling planes, and in the hangar helping to build them. Most important, she learned to fly. She took lessons, got her license, and went up every chance she got.

The only downside was that taking the time to practice flying left her with *hours* of office work to catch up on every night. She'd sit at her desk, picturing the fun she was missing, the hot jazz bands and new Hollywood movies. But could she seriously imagine wanting any other life? Not really.

And anyway, the most interesting people weren't at nightclubs or theaters. They were at the airport.

One day at the field, Louise met a young engineer and former army flier named Herb Thaden—in her words, "tall, blonde, attractive." Herb was working on an innovative all-metal plane of his own design. They had a lot to talk about. Trying to play it cool, like she didn't care one way or the other, Louise asked Herb if he'd like to test out a new plane Travel Air was building. He said he'd love to.

She got in the front seat, letting him take the controls in the back—not something she would do for just anyone. The flight was going fine until, high above Oakland, a loud *HISSSSS* started shooting from the engine. Then the radiator cap shot into the sky. Steaming water sprayed from the front of the plane.

Herb brought them in for a quick landing, just in time. As soon as they touched down, the overheated engine locked up, belching black smoke and the stench of melting rubber.

Louise and Herb jumped to the ground and stood together as a fire truck, siren blaring, raced toward the burning plane. Herb offered to cover the damage to the engine, which turned out to be a whopping $300. Louise insisted on paying the bill herself.

For two people obsessed with flying, it was a pretty good first date. A few months later, they got married.

Ruth Elder's life was going in a very different direction.

The fearless girl who'd once leapt from the roof of a shed onto the back of her running horse now sat all day at the receptionist's desk in a dental office in Lakeland, Florida, listening to people complain about their teeth. She earned just seventeen dollars a week. She went home to a one-room apartment. She was stuck in an unhappy marriage. She was twenty-three and hated her life.

The one thing that kept Ruth going was flying. Whenever she could scrape together a few bucks, she'd race to the airport for a lesson.

"When I passed my solo test, I was the proudest girl in Florida," she remembered, "and I secretly resolved I would attempt to cross the Atlantic."

This was 1927, when the idea of flying a plane across three thousand miles of ocean sounded like something from science fiction, as new and as thrilling as spaceflight would be to people in the 1950s, or a trip to Mars would be today. Keep in mind, it was dangerous to cross a *lake* in the planes of the 1920s. Out over the open ocean, a pilot was truly and terrifyingly alone, out of touch and beyond help in a way that could never happen now. Pilots kept trying to cross the Atlantic Ocean—and dying at sea.

Finally, in May 1927, a twenty-five-year-old airmail pilot named Charles Lindbergh rocketed to world fame with a 33½-hour, nonstop solo flight from New York to Paris.

Ruth Elder wanted in.

"I'm going to fly across the Atlantic just as soon as the weather is right," she vowed. When people reminded her that she was a dental receptionist with limited flight experience, Ruth was unmoved. "What difference does it make whether people think I'm going to try it or not? I know I am."

Her original idea was to fly solo. She was able to convince sponsors to provide money for the attempt—she could never have saved enough on her paltry salary—but her backers insisted she fly with a copilot. She asked her flight instructor, George Haldeman.

"Girl, are you crazy?" he snorted.

She assured him she was not. He agreed to come along.

Ruth's husband did not approve. Her mother begged her to drop the dangerous dream. That summer's newspapers were filled with tragic stories about Mildred Doran, a twenty-two-year-old fifth-grade teacher from Michigan whose plane disappeared over the Pacific Ocean while attempting a flight from California to Hawaii, and about Princess Anne of Löwenstein-Wertheim, a sixty-three-year-old English adventurer who vanished trying to fly the Atlantic from Europe to America.

Ruth Elder knew the stories. She was unfazed.

Ruth had grown up watching her parents suffer the strain of supporting eight kids. She'd already worked a series of low-paying jobs in stores and offices, and there weren't many opportunities for a woman to go further. Now, for the first time, she had a clear vision of how to turn her life around. This flight—if she could pull it off—was her ticket out. She'd be the first woman to fly across the ocean, an instant celebrity. Maybe she could find work as a pilot, maybe even land a movie contract.

And if she couldn't pull it off?

"I know that it's a long chance," Ruth Elder told reporters. "If I win, then I'm on top. If I lose—well, I've lived, and that's that."

RACING ACROSS THE ATLANTIC

Elder and Haldeman picked a Stinson Detroiter for the Atlantic attempt, a powerful plane with side-by-side pilot seats in an enclosed cockpit. With a sharp eye for marketing, Ruth gave the plane a catchy name and had it painted in script along the side of the cabin: *American Girl*.

In October 1927, she and George flew to their starting point, Roosevelt Field in Long Island, New York, the field Lindbergh had left from on his historic flight to Paris. Reporters gathered to cover what was becoming a huge national story. Ruth enjoyed the attention, but she found it annoying to be pestered with questions no male pilot had to face.

"What will you wear on the flight?"

"What I've got on, I suppose." She was wearing flying clothes: pants and a men's shirt.

"Do you only want to fly to Paris because you are a girl?"

"Well, they've got pretty evening gowns there, I hear," Ruth said, flashing a sarcastic smile. "I've never been to Europe—might as well go this way."

"Are you engaged to Captain Haldeman?"

"Say, listen," George cut in. "I'm married."

American Girl took off on the afternoon of October 11. Elder and Haldeman watched the sun set as they passed over Nantucket Island, the last land they'd see before Europe. They watched the rising moon light a sparkling path on the black water.

The press followed Ruth Elder everywhere—even on her test flight around New York City.

Thirty-six hours later, there was no sign of them.

In Elder's hometown of Anniston, Alabama, her parents, two sisters, and five brothers waited by the telephone. It didn't ring. The Elders couldn't afford a radio, but a friend brought one over. There were no updates on the news.

LOST AT SEA, declared one Paris headline.

GIRL FLYER'S MOTHER IS NEAR COLLAPSE was the headline in the *Anniston Star*.

But *American Girl* was still in the air. Barely.

The first twelve hours had been smooth and easy. Ruth and George took turns at the controls, singing to stay alert. Then things began to go wrong.

The sky ahead turned into a wall of gray clouds. Lightning flashed as they slammed into a massive storm. Wind tossed the plane like a toy, and sleet pounded the cockpit. Fighting the controls to keep the plane level, Ruth watched ice form on the edges of the windshield. Nothing in her brief training had prepared her for this kind of flying.

George had the training, and he looked worried—which told her she should worry, too.

He turned to her and asked how she was doing.

"Fine!" she said. "George, we'll get through it soon."

He agreed. They both knew they were lying to each other.

After six exhausting hours of battling the storm, they sailed into a patch of clear sky and moonlight—only to see oil spraying from the motor and splattering the right wing. Through their long second night in the air, Ruth shined a flashlight on the oil-pressure gauge, watching the needle steadily dropping.

"The old motor don't sound right, Ruth," George said. "And I don't think the gauge is lying."

They tried to talk about other things, but the conversation fizzled. They tried to eat but wound up throwing their sandwiches out the window. The combined effects of caffeine tablets and terror kept them wide-awake.

By sunrise, the motor was making an evil pounding sound. There was no land in sight. There couldn't be much oil left in the engine, and they were running out of gasoline.

Then, with the motor making a deafening death rattle, they spotted a ship. It was their one chance.

George splashed the plane down in the choppy ocean, and, to speed their escape, Ruth grabbed a knife and slashed a hole in the canvas-covered side of the cabin. They scrambled out as cold water rushed in, each clinging to one wing of the sinking plane as sailors from the ship raced toward them in a lifeboat.

A reporter from the *Anniston Star* ran to the Elder home with a telegram—Ruth and George were alive! They'd gone down at sea but were safely aboard a Dutch oil tanker and heading for land.

"Ruth is a mighty smart girl and all that," Mr. Elder said with tears in his eyes, "but the young lady has just a bit more nerve than is good for her."

Mrs. Elder, who'd suffered weeks of sleepless nights since hearing of her daughter's plan, was finally smiling. "You mustn't say that," she told her husband. "Ruth is all right. She's the finest daughter in the world, and she's the greatest little woman ever, even if I am her own mother and say it."

Ruth's teenage brothers had the best lines.

"Boots is a whale of a girl," said Hughey Elder, using his sister's family nickname. "Gee, she must have had fun on that trip."

"Ruth is the goods, all right," added Alfred. "That girl knows her onion!"

Bells chimed in Anniston. Fire sirens blared in Ruth Elder's honor.

Beyond her hometown, the reaction was mixed.

For her historic flight—the longest ever by a woman, the longest over open water by *anyone*, man or woman—Ruth Elder became, as one article put it, "one of the most scolded young women of her time."

"A woman had no business to attempt such a flight," another paper proclaimed, noting with disdain that she had a husband in Florida. "If Ruth has any sense left, she will join him now and keep house for him."

"Hereafter, American girls will stay on the ground," yet another preached, "or at least do their flying over land."

But Ruth Elder could laugh it off. Because her plan worked. It worked perfectly.

She was an instant celebrity. Her smiling face was on the front page of newspapers everywhere. The colorful bands she wore in her hair were dubbed "Ruth Ribbons," sparking a nationwide fad. Before the flight, she'd never earned twenty dollars in a week. Now she was offered contracts to endorse products, contracts to appear on stage and in movies—deals worth $250,000, well over $3.5 million in today's money.

It was fun, and she jumped at the chance to buy her parents a new house.

Ruth Elder in the cockpit of the *American Girl*.

But Ruth Elder still dreamed of flying. "I expect to try another trans-Atlantic flight," she announced, "if no other woman accomplishes one meanwhile."

Other women definitely intended to accomplish one meanwhile.

A pilot named Frances Grayson tried next. Her plane went down somewhere near Cape Cod. Her body was never found.

Next, a woman named Amy Phipps Guest bought her own plane, hoping to make the flight. When her family pressured her to drop the plan, she turned to George Putnam, a publisher of adventure books, and asked if he knew any women who might be willing to take her place in the plane.

Putnam liked the idea. The story could sell a ton of books, *if* he could find just the right woman. She had to know how to fly. She had to be marketable: articulate and photogenic.

His first thought was another Ruth, a young pilot—and future Women's Air Derby contestant—named Ruth Nichols. Nichols had recently made headline news with the first nonstop flight from New York City to Miami. She was off flying around the country, though, and Putnam didn't want to wait.

He made a few phone calls, and a friend of his in Boston, Hilton Railey, said he knew of someone who might be perfect. Railey offered to give her a call.

The telephone rang in Denison House, a settlement house in Boston. Children from the neighborhood, who came for after-school activities and lessons, were racing through the halls, shouting and laughing. One of the kids picked up the phone.

He listened for a moment, then called out: "Phone for you, Miss Earhart!"

"Tell 'em I'm busy!"

As she really was. Amelia Earhart had moved to Boston a few years before and was working at Denison House, teaching English to adult immigrants and leading after-school classes for their kids. The afternoon was her busiest time. At the moment, she was surrounded by dozens of students, trying to get everyone into the right rooms.

The boy at the phone passed on the message, then listened again.

"He says it's important to speak with you."

Annoyed, Earhart grabbed the receiver.

"Hello," she heard a man's voice say. "You don't know me, but my name is Railey—Captain H. H. Railey."

He asked if she was interested in doing something in aviation. Something hazardous. She wanted more information. He refused to give any over the phone, suggesting they meet at his office that evening. Amelia was intrigued. She said she'd be there. She still loved to fly and went up on weekends when she had the money. She'd always thought of flying as a hobby, though. That night, in Railey's office, her future—and our history—took a turn.

"I might as well lay the cards on the table," he said the moment she sat down. "Would you fly the Atlantic?"

"Yes."

It was that fast. As she'd later explain, "How could I refuse such a shining adventure?"

But first she had to convince the men organizing the flight she was right for the job.

Earhart went to New York City to meet George Putnam and his team. As they talked, she found herself in an absurd position, one no male pilot would ever have to face. She wanted to impress these men, get them to like her—but not like her *too* much.

"If they liked me too well," she explained, "they might be loath to drown me."

She played it just right. Putnam especially loved that Amelia Earhart looked a bit like Charles Lindbergh.

With rival Atlantic attempts in the works, the team raced in secret to prepare. The crew would consist of Amelia Earhart and two men: a pilot named Bill Stultz and Lou Gordon, a mechanic. Stultz would get $20,000 for the flight, and Gordon $5,000.

Earhart was offered the immortal glory of being the first woman to cross the Atlantic. No cash.

She insisted, though, on doing some of the flying. No woman had ever crossed the ocean by air as a passenger *or* pilot, and either would be a big story. But the idea of making history as a passenger did not appeal to Amelia.

At a hangar in East Boston, Amy Phipps Guest's Fokker F7 trimotor monoplane, *Friendship*, was adapted for the Atlantic attempt. Mechanics pulled out the seats—there was room in the enclosed cabin for eight passengers—and installed extra fuel tanks. They added pontoons so the plane could land on water. The tops of the wings were painted bright orange to make *Friendship* more visible in the all-too-likely event it went down at sea.

Amelia Earhart kept the flight secret even from her family. She wrote out a will and put it in a safe-deposit box in her bank. She wrote letters to her parents, to be opened only if she did not return.

"Dear Dad," said one. "Hooray for the last grand adventure! I wish I had won, but it was worthwhile anyway. You know that."

Muriel Earhart—who'd once helped her big sister build a roller coaster in their yard—found out about the flight from a newspaper headline on June 17, 1928.

GIRL PILOT DARES THE ATLANTIC

Friendship had just taken off, and the story was finally out. Reporters banged on the door of the Boston home Muriel shared with her mother, shouting questions, demanding old photos of Amelia.

At Denison House, kids pestered the staff with questions:

"Where is Miss Earhart now?"

"Is she still flying?"

She was. In the cabin of *Friendship*, Amelia huddled in the dark, cramped space between the front seats and the extra fuel tanks. The plane wobbled and bounced, climbing through storms to over ten thousand feet. From that height, she looked down at landscapes of clouds and light, views few human eyes had seen. She watched in awe, jotting notes in the flight log:

"The sun is sinking behind a limitless sea of fog, and we have a bright rainbow."

"The highest peaks of the fog mountains are tinted pink with the setting sun."

For the next five hours the sky was dark and the air was rough. Radioactive radium in the cockpit dials lit the cabin in a faint green glow. The fliers sipped coffee and passed around hunks of pemmican—dried meat—which Earhart described as "cold lard with dark, unidentified lumps floating in it." Amelia took a turn up front but never got the controls—she had no experience flying with so little visibility, using instruments alone to keep the plane level.

By sunrise, they were down to a few hours of fuel. The port side motor was coughing. Cold rain dripped into the cabin as Stultz took them down through the clouds, looking for an opening. They finally got low enough to see the ocean. But this told them nothing about where they were, or how far from land. The crew could *estimate* their location by calculating how long they'd been flying and in what direction, taking into account the plane's speed and the speed and direction of the wind. But a rough guess was the best anyone could do.

A rough guess said the coast of Ireland should be coming into view. There was no land in sight. They were down to an hour of fuel. The port engine was cutting on and off.

"Where are we? Are we beaten?"

Those were the thoughts racing through Earhart's mind when she spotted a ship in the water below. Stultz saw it, too, dove toward it, and circled. Amelia dashed off a note, asking the ship's captain to paint the coordinates of his position on the deck. She put the paper in a bag, added two oranges for weight, opened the hatch in the floor, and aimed for the ship.

She missed. The bag splashed into the ocean. It was a nearly impossible shot.

They could try landing near the ship, but Stultz thought the water was too choppy. The only other option was to go on, knowing they may not see another ship. Knowing they could run out of fuel at any moment. Knowing the plane's life jackets and rubber life raft had been scrapped at the last second to save weight.

Earhart recalled no debate. "We all favored sticking to the course."

They flew on in tense silence. Stultz held the plane at five hundred feet to stay below the clouds.

"We could see only a few miles of water, which melted into the grayness on all sides," Earhart later wrote.

For half an hour, they saw nothing else. Then a good sign—a small fishing boat. Then a few small boats.

And then a misty blue shape came into view. It looked a lot like the clouds they'd been seeing the whole trip, but as they flew closer, they made out a cliff, sea splashing at its base. And there were farms nearby, roads, a town!

Stultz set the plane down in a small port. *Friendship* bobbed on calm water, half a mile from land.

"20 hrs 40 mins," Earhart wrote in the flight log, noting the time since takeoff. "*Friendship* down safely in harbor of _____."

She left that last part blank. They had no idea where they were.

PUSHING
LIMITS

No one in the town of Burry Port, Wales, seemed too curious about the visitors. They looked out at the plane that had just landed but had no idea where it had come from or that it had made any sort of special flight. They continued about their business.

"I'll get a boat," Amelia Earhart said.

She leaned out of the *Friendship* cabin, waving a white handkerchief at three men working on a railroad track near the waterfront.

The men waved to her. Then went back to work.

Finally, after an hour, people started rowing out in boats.

That's when the *Friendship* crew found out they'd reached the west coast of Great Britain. They'd passed Ireland without even seeing it. But they'd done it; they'd crossed the Atlantic Ocean.

With that one flight, Amelia Earhart went from unknown social worker to international celebrity. The next few weeks, both in Britain and back home, were a head-spinning series of photographs, interviews, speeches, lunches, dinners, parades. She wrote a book about the flight for George

Not a pose for those afraid of heights—Amelia Earhart on the roof of a London hotel.

Putnam. *McCall's Magazine* offered her a job as aviation editor. Reluctantly, she appeared in an advertisement for Lucky Strike cigarettes—only agreeing so her *Friendship* crewmates could earn money from the ad.

When the ad appeared, *McCall's* withdrew its offer. A woman who smoked was seen as a bit rebellious, a bit too free from traditional ladylike behavior. The men at the magazine did not approve. Angry letters flooded Earhart's mailbox:

"Cigarette smoking is to be expected from any woman who cuts her hair like a man's and who wears trousers in public."

And: "I suppose you *drink* also."

Earhart didn't even like smoking—though she was all for pushing limits on what women could do. Only one thing about the Atlantic flight really bothered her.

"What's the matter?" Hilton Railey asked when he saw her after the flight. "Aren't you excited?"

"It was a grand experience, but all I did was lie on my tummy and take pictures of the ocean," she said. "I was just baggage, like a sack of potatoes."

Being first across the ocean made her the most famous female pilot in the world, but she hadn't actually *flown*. Amelia Earhart was left with the nagging feeling that, at some point soon, she would have to prove herself as a pilot.

Pancho Barnes was proving herself as a pilot. Though not in a way that everyone appreciated.

One Sunday morning in Pasadena, California, the Reverend Rankin Barnes stood before his congregation in church, head bowed in prayer, when the peaceful silence was shattered by the growl of an engine. The obnoxious roar grew louder and louder. It seemed to be coming from the sky. The whole building began to shake. The reverend stepped outside and looked up.

An airplane was circling the church steeple. In the pilot seat was the reverend's wife. She was flying so low he could clearly see that she was howling with joy.

At twenty-seven, Pancho Barnes had finally found herself. She built her entire life around flying. She took jobs as a stunt pilot in air shows and Hollywood movies. She hung around airfields all over Southern California, servicing her own plane, swapping flying stories with fellow pilots, striking matches on the seat of her jeans to light her cigars, devouring what she called "cannibal sandwiches"—raw hamburger meat and onion between two slices of bread. She'd even fly liquor smugglers over the Mexican border and back for ten dollars a trip. To Pancho, the fact that this was during Prohibition,

when it was illegal to make or sell alcoholic beverages in the United States, was all part of the fun.

"We swaggered a bit in our helmets, goggles, white scarf, and boots," she fondly recalled of her flying adventures. "It was truly the golden age of flying, and we were the cast."

Pancho had burned through most of the money she'd inherited from her wealthy parents, but so what? Why slow down now?

"I don't give a darn about saving it," she told a friend. "Anything—money or whatever. Now I'm here. I want to live and like it. Why should I wait? I might be dead tomorrow. The next minute even."

Marvel Crosson was proving herself, too, in a quieter way. She was living in Fairbanks, Alaska, in a log cabin with no indoor plumbing. On Thanksgiving, it was thirty below zero. And then winter set in.

It was a dream come true.

Joe Crosson had taken a job as a pilot in Fairbanks. In the fall of 1927, after selling the plane she and Joe had built in their backyard, Marvel joined him in Alaska. They fixed planes together. They flew deliveries of food, mail, and lifesaving medicine to remote mining camps all over Alaska.

"It takes hours to get your planes warmed up," Marvel wrote of the extreme conditions. "Even the hangars and sheds are cold. You have to work in mittens or your hands will freeze fast to the metal parts."

When her open-cockpit plane got airborne, it *really* got chilly. Marvel flew in a fur suit, cheeks icing over in wind-chills that hit a hundred below, peering over the side of the plane to navigate by landmarks like mountains and frozen rivers. There was no margin for error. If something went wrong and she had to put the plane down in the roadless wilderness, she might be a month's walk from the nearest town.

As the first woman to fly in Alaska, Marvel Crosson was featured in articles in a few small newspapers. Writers described her radiant smile, her contagious love of flying, her absolute conviction that women could fly as well as men, and her incredible technical knowledge.

"Even Joe admits," noted one paper, "that his sister is the better mechanic."

They gave her ridiculous nicknames like "Flying Grocery Girl" and "Pollyanna of the North." A small price to pay, Marvel figured. She was working with Joe, flying for a living, getting better every day. A letter she wrote at this time to a former high school teacher ends with a line that says it all:

Marvel Crosson (right) in Alaska with her friend Lillian Osborne. Lillian would later marry Marvel's brother, Joe.

"Well, Miss Hagen, I guess I'd best ring off before I bore you to death with flying—but I guess you can guess it's all I know, really."

By the summer of 1928, Louise McPhetridge—Louise Thaden, since her marriage to Herb—was ready to test for her transport license. This was the ultimate goal for pilots who were serious about working in aviation. With a transport license, you could fly passengers for money and teach flight lessons.

Louise was defying both odds and tradition. Women were expected to give up their jobs when they got married—only 10 percent of married American women worked outside the home in the 1920s. Many of the country's major employers, including automaker Henry Ford, wanted to keep it that way. "I pay our women well," Ford said, "so they can dress attractively and get married." Some women dreamed of the day when they, like men, could "have it all," career *and* family. For most, it was a distant fantasy.

Louise Thaden saw a way to make it happen, but she needed that transport license.

She had the required two hundred hours of flight time. She aced the four-hour written exam. The final step was the notoriously challenging flight test. When the big day came, Louise stood on the edge of the Oakland airfield, nervously watching a young man take the test before her. He flunked.

"Come back in three months," the flight inspector told him as they climbed out of the plane.

The inspector strode toward Louise. He had a fierce gaze, a thick mustache, and a carefully cultivated reputation for intimidating young pilots.

"Your ship ready?"

"Yes, sir," she said, then cringed. She'd squeaked like a baby frog.

"Let's go," he grunted. "I'm tired."

They walked to her plane.

"You are the first woman I've tested for a transport rating," the inspector said. "Because you are, I'm going to be particularly hard on you. You understand why?"

She shook her head no.

"A man can get into difficulty and I won't be blamed. But if *you* do!"

It was the best possible thing he could have said.

They took off. Instead of being distracted by her anger, it focused her, and she flew better than she'd ever flown. She climbed and spun, flipped and dove. She cut the engine at three thousand feet and glided in for a feather-soft dead-stick landing.

The inspector looked at her and said, "You'll do."

But she could see that he was trying not to smile.

"I could have kissed him," she later said. "Mustache and all."

Louise Thaden blew two weeks' pay on a party, and with good reason. Just a little over a year since leaving Wichita, she'd become the first woman on the West Coast to earn a transport license. As she'd later say, "I was beginning to feel I was a 'hot' pilot."

It was a dangerous way to think.

Louise Thaden spent the afternoon of August 19, 1928, at a celebration for the opening of an airport on Alameda Island. Near sunset, as people started heading home, she saw that a friend and fellow pilot, Sandy Sanders, was in no condition to fly. He'd had a few drinks and needed a ride back to Oakland.

"Clothed in my newborn conceit," Louise recalled, "I volunteered."

She topped off the gas tank and went through preflight checks on Sandy's plane. She warmed up the engine, and they took off for the short flight. As the plane climbed, Louise watched the needle of the temperature gauge slide dangerously high, two hundred degrees and still rising. At four hundred feet above the ground, the engine quit.

The sudden silence was terrifying.

Thaden tried to turn and glide back toward the Alameda field, but the plane tipped on its side and went into a downward spin. Louise sat in the back seat, gripping the useless controls, thinking it was taking an eerily long time to fall four hundred feet. She would never remember hitting the ground.

She opened her eyes in the back of a car. People were leaning over her, making sounds, words maybe, but she couldn't understand.

Next, she was in a wheelchair, being pushed down a brightly lit hospital hallway. Her leg throbbed. She touched her pounding head, and her fingers came away sticky with blood. As she passed the open door of a room, she saw Sandy inside, lying on a table. Doctors were sewing up his head.

Next, she was in a bed, trying to figure out how she got there. A doctor was cutting off her boot.

Suddenly, it was morning. A friend from the airport came in.

"The plane is a complete washout," he said. "It's a miracle you weren't hurt worse—your feet and legs went clear through the floorboards."

Sandy, he told her, was dead.

Thaden felt hot tears slipping from her closed eyes. She opened her eyes and looked out the window. A sunny day, a normal day. How could everything look so normal?

Barely able to prop herself up with crutches, she went to the funeral against doctors' orders. Her body ached, but that was bearable compared with the deeper pain. "There was an ache in my heart, a bitter condemnation," she'd later say. "The torture of remorse ate at my brain, and it left scars."

She went back to work. Pilot friends stopped by her office to offer sympathy. They told her not to blame herself, there was nothing she could have done to keep that plane in the air.

But she *did* blame herself. She played the crash over and over in her head, tormenting herself for trying to turn the plane around after the engine had failed at low altitude—exactly what instructors warn students *never* to do. If she'd tried landing straight ahead, would the crash have been as bad? Would Sandy be alive?

There was no way to know.

No way to stop wondering.

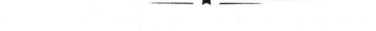

"A pilot who says he has never been frightened in an airplane is, I'm afraid, lying."

That was Louise Thaden's assessment after a lifetime in aviation. At twenty-three, things didn't look so clear-cut. Weren't the best pilots supposed to be fearless? It took her a while to realize that no one was fearless. But some people were brave. They got scared sometimes, and they climbed into the cockpit anyway.

That was Louise Thaden. She didn't just get back into the air, she pushed herself to be better and smarter and—when she felt ready—to take her place among the country's top pilots.

In December 1928, Thaden set her sights on the women's altitude record, which stood at 19,400 feet, held by an Irish pilot, Lady Mary Heath. The Travel Air mechanics were behind Louise all the way. They modified a plane for the extreme stress of high-altitude flight. They added extra fuel tanks and arranged to borrow oxygen equipment from a local hospital. A doctor brought over a metal tank and a gas mask for her cockpit.

"You know how to use oxygen, don't you?" the doctor asked Louise.

She did not. She just knew there wasn't enough of it to breathe at the altitude she was hoping to reach. He showed her how to put the mask on and how to open and close the valve on the tank with a pair of pliers.

"You must be very careful," he said. "If you don't get sufficient oxygen, you'll pass out."

She asked what would happen if she got too much.

"You'll pass out."

Louise Thaden with the oxygen tank she'd need to reach record heights.

"How do I know whether I'm taking too much or too little?"

"Well, that's hard to tell," the doctor said. "Your reactions will slow up, only you won't realize it. Watch yourself carefully."

With this less-than-reassuring advice in mind, Thaden pulled on a fur-lined flying suit and climbed into her plane. It was a sunny morning in

Oakland, and she immediately started sweating. But she'd need the suit. Air temperate drops about five degrees with every one thousand feet of elevation.

She took off and circled the field in an aggressive climb for over an hour, watching the altimeter needle spin: five thousand feet, then ten thousand. At fifteen thousand feet, her thermometer read two degrees above zero.

It was getting hard to breathe. She put on the gas mask and opened the valve just a bit. The oxygen helped, but doubts flew through her mind: Was she getting too much oxygen? Too little? Were her reactions slowing down? She didn't think so—but hadn't the doctor said she wouldn't notice?

She kept climbing, pulling back on the stick, engine roaring as the plane struggled to generate lift in the thin air. At twenty thousand feet, the temperature was minus twenty. The moisture in her breath condensed, dripped down her chin, and froze in icy streaks. She felt fine, though, and the view was spectacular. Oakland airport was a postage stamp. San Francisco Bay was a puddle. She opened the oxygen valve another fraction of an inch.

"Come on, baby," she shouted to her plane. "Just a hundred feet more! You can do it—just a hundred—"

That's when she passed out.

RACING FOR RECORDS

Thaden's plane tipped forward and went into a nosedive.

Her eyes snapped open. A painful screech rang inside her head. The altimeter was blurry at first, but she could see the needle unwinding, spinning fast. Ripping off the ice-caked oxygen mask, she gulped cold air into her lungs. She gripped the stick with numb and clumsy fingers and pulled out of the dive.

As she circled lower and lower, her vision cleared. The screech in her head faded. An hour and a half after taking off, she was safely back on the ground.

For record attempts, the National Aeronautical Association required planes to carry an extra set of instruments, which the pilot could not see. The instruments were shipped to the National Bureau of Standards in Washington, DC, where they were unsealed and read. The process took three agonizing weeks.

Finally, in early January 1929, the official reading was announced. Louise Thaden's top altitude was 20,270 feet. A world record.

The men's altitude record was well over thirty thousand feet—but male pilots had the advantage of flying powerful military planes for their record attempts. It made sense for women, flying smaller, civilian aircraft, to have their own records. Louise Thaden would challenge the top male fliers directly one day. For now, she was happy to be alive, and proud.

And far from satisfied.

"I can establish a higher altitude mark than this one," Thaden told the *Oakland Tribune*.

She'd have to if she wanted to stay on top. The intense rivalry between top female fliers was just beginning to heat up.

Bobbi Trout jumped right into the race for records.

Before sunrise on the morning of January 2, 1929, Trout took off from a Los Angeles airport in a plane weighted down with extra fuel tanks. Trout had her sights set on a record for endurance. The goal of an endurance flight was simple: stay in the air as long as possible. The pilot had to fly alone. She had to take off and land from the same field. The women's endurance record stood at eight hours and six minutes. Bobbi was sure she could beat it.

"Once I make up my mind to do something," she told a friend, "I do it or know the reason why."

As the sun rose, Bobbi fought to control her plane. The weight of the extra fuel made Bobbi's plane wobble and swerve; if she lost focus, even for a second, she'd slip out of control. The flying got easier as she burned fuel. She ate five sandwiches, cruised past the record by mid-afternoon, watched the sun set, and landed in the dark with an empty tank of gas, twelve hours and eleven minutes after takeoff.

Family and friends ran onto the field shouting, "You did it! You did it!"

Reporters raced to Bobbi's plane as she taxied to a stop. Photographers' flashbulbs popped in her exhausted eyes.

"I always hated working around the house, and I always liked mechanical things," Trout told the crowd. "I'm glad I stayed up long, because now maybe I won't have to wash dishes."

Bobbi's record didn't survive the month of January. A seventeen-year-old pilot named Elinor Smith made sure of that.

"In an age when girls were supposed to be seen and not heard," Smith would later say, "look beautiful, and occasionally faint, I didn't seem to fit in anywhere."

But there was *one* place she felt at home—the airport. Elinor spent her childhood hanging around Long Island's Roosevelt Field, wearing her brother's sneakers and leather jacket, dreaming of flight. She took flying lessons with a pillow behind her back so she could reach the rudder. She earned her license at sixteen, becoming the youngest pilot in the world, man or woman.

A year later, in October 1928, Elinor Smith made front-page news by flying low along New York City's East River, swerving around ships and skimming ten feet above the water as she zipped *under* the Queensboro Bridge, the Williamsburg Bridge, the Manhattan Bridge, and the Brooklyn Bridge. To celebrate, she circled the Statue of Liberty before heading home.

Lots of pilots had talked about flying under these four bridges, bragged they were going to. But no one had ever actually *done* it. It was an incredibly tricky piece of flying.

Also illegal. Elinor was ordered to report to City Hall.

She showed up with her dad and stood in the mayor's assistant's office, her stomach churning, terrified she was about to lose the thing she treasured most in life: her pilot's license.

Mayor Jimmy Walker strode in, glanced at the teenager, and asked what she was doing there.

"You remember—we sent for her," his assistant said.

"Why?"

"Well, Mr. Mayor, she flew under all the East River bridges."

Walker did a looping double take, like something from a comedy routine. "You can't mean that this child is the careless daredevil we are supposed to chastise publicly?"

The assistant said, "I'm afraid so."

Mayor Walker tried to appear angry. It didn't work. He was so impressed by Elinor's flying skill he let her off with a slap on the wrist—a ten-day suspension of her license.

Smith was soon back in the air, gunning for Bobbi Trout's endurance record. She went up on the frigid afternoon of January 30, 1929, flying circles over Long Island through the night, singing aloud for the last five hours to stay awake. When she landed, her legs were so stiff she had to be lifted out of the plane. The coffee in her thermos was frozen solid.

But she had the record: thirteen hours, sixteen minutes.

And something more than the record. Smith saw articles suggesting that record-setting pilots like her were advancing the cause of women's rights, and she hoped it was true. "It pleased me that anyone thought I had struck a blow for change."

"Gosh, I hate to take the record away from Elinor Smith," Bobbi Trout said when she heard of Smith's flight. "But I have to do it. I just loaned it to her for a couple of weeks."

On February 11, Trout smashed Smith's record.

TOMBOY STAYS IN AIR 17 HOURS TO AVOID WASHING DISHES, announced a Los Angeles newspaper.

Louise Thaden set a new mark in mid-March, with a solo flight of over twenty-two hours.

In April, Elinor Smith promptly upped the record to twenty-six hours.

The world's youngest pilot, man or woman—Elinor Smith.

Marvel Crosson could not possibly stay away.

After following the record race in the newspapers, Marvel was back in California in search of new flying adventures. And new records.

"I hope Bobbi will set a new endurance record," she told the *Los Angeles Times*. "You know, I might even try to break that, too, later on, and it would be nice to have a new mark to shoot at. However, I am anxious to try for the altitude record first."

On May 28, in her fur-lined flight suit and boots from Alaska, Marvel took off from Clover Field in Santa Monica and started to climb. She rose into sub-zero temperatures, breathing oxygen through a pipe and tube installed in her plane by the Los Angeles Fire Department.

"I climbed the ship," she said after the two-hour flight, "until it reached a point where it just seemed to be hanging in the air by the propeller and making no altitude."

Shivering and light-headed, she leaned forward to turn on a second oxygen tank—and her head swam. She was about to black out. Time to start down.

By the time she landed, her entire body was numb.

"Gee," she told her cheering family and friends, "it was cold up there."

The plane's sealed instruments were sent to Washington. A telegram came back with the official reading. Marvel hadn't broken Louise Thaden's record. She'd shattered it. The women's altitude mark now stood at 23,996 feet—more than four and a half miles above the ground.

NEW STAR OF THE CLOUDS, declared the *New York Times*.

Marvel Crosson appeared in newsreels shown before movies. She was featured in advertisements for airplanes and oil companies. Women started recognizing her on the street. Many were inspired by Marvel. Many were confused.

"Why don't you stop flying?" she was often asked. "Why don't you do like the rest of us?"

"Flying is the greatest thing in the world," she'd explain. "I intend to prove that a woman can do a man's work in the air."

To which some women would say, "How extraordinary!"

Or they'd silently shake their heads, smiling politely.

Marvel left it at that. Not everyone needed to understand.

That spring, she got engaged to a pilot named Emory Bronte, who was famous for making one of the first flights from California to Hawaii. Approached by newspapers for a comment, Bronte refused to confirm the story.

"A long-distance flyer shouldn't be married," he said. "When he flies to distant lands, he should never leave his girl behind; in fact, he shouldn't make such attempts if he is married."

Marvel and Emory really *were* engaged, but they preferred to keep it private. They were both focused on new challenges in the air. What Marvel really wanted was to test herself directly against the best fliers in the country. There was only one way to do that.

"I want to race," she told a friend, "just like the men."

She was about to get her chance.

Marvel and Joe and the airplane they built in their backyard.

THE WOMEN'S AIR DERBY

Almost as soon as humans figured out how to get flying machines into the air—and long before they figured out how to keep them there—pilots began challenging each other to races in the sky.

In the summer of 1909, hundreds of thousands gathered in Reims, France, to see the world's first air races. The scene was like something from a jousting tournament in the Middle Ages: huge crowds in fine clothes, thrills and peril, with the role of knights in armor played by dashing pilots in goggles and leather coats. In an instant, a new sport was born.

In the meet's main event, two laps around a six-mile course marked with pylons, American plane builder Glenn Curtiss took first place, averaging forty-seven miles per hour. In a rematch the following year at Belmont Park on Long Island, French pilot Alfred Leblanc was speeding to the finish line, well out in front, when he ran out of gas, crashed into a telegraph pole, and was lucky to limp away from his shattered plane.

An estimated half a million fans turned out for the start of the Circuit of Europe race in 1911, a three-week challenge, with stops in France, Belgium, the Netherlands, and England. Forty-three pilots started the race. Nine finished. Pilots lost their way and landed at the wrong field. Sometimes in the wrong country. Engines failed in the air. Planes caught fire or broke apart on landing. Three of the racers were killed.

In the 1920s, as air racing grew into a major sport in the United States, the pattern continued. Races drew big crowds, top pilots, cutting-edge planes, and massive media attention. Crashes were part of the game.

And, just like a tournament of knights, women were expected to stand aside and cheer. The competition was for men only.

There were *always* crack-ups in long-distance air races, often fatal ones. The danger only heightened the drama—as long as the pilots crashing and dying were men. Race organizers worried that if women were allowed to race and crashed—which was inevitable—it would be a national scandal. Races avoided this risk by excluding women.

"A man can damage a plane and hardly a word be said," one airplane manufacturer told Amelia Earhart, "but that doesn't apply when sister stubs her toe."

Earhart and other female pilots were sick of this attitude. When had they ever asked for sympathy or special treatment? They knew the risks and were eager to compete.

Elizabeth McQueen, a fifty-one-year-old pilot and tireless promoter of flying opportunities for women, added her voice to the calls for a women's air race. McQueen arranged a meeting with the organizers of the 1929 National Air Races—the biggest event of the year in aviation—and urged the addition of a women-only cross-country race. The nine-day race would start on the West Coast and wind through the Southwest and Midwest, with the finish line at the National Air Races in Cleveland in late August.

Cliff Henderson, director of the National Air Races, actually liked the idea.

Sure, it would be a huge risk. This was a time when articles in serious aviation magazines routinely printed comments such as: "Women are by nature impulsive and scatter-brained." And: "Women pilots are too emotional, vain, and frivolous to fly, and are hazards to themselves and others." Henderson knew that if women were allowed to race, the entire country would be watching. Many would be eager to pounce, just *waiting* for something to go wrong so they could scream, "I told you so!"

On the other hand, the entire country would be watching.

A women's cross-country race would be headline news *everywhere* for nine days, drawing curious crowds to every airfield along the course. Besides, Henderson was well aware that pilots like Marvel Crosson and Louise Thaden could fly as well as anyone. A national race would prove it.

It was agreed. The first Women's Air Derby would be held in August.

Two things happened immediately. First, the usual pushback against anything new. As Elizabeth McQueen put it, "The public press generally censured this outburst of 'feminism' in a man's world."

Second, pilots raced to sign up.

The first official entrant was Marvel Crosson.

When Bobbi Trout was asked if she'd be interested, she shouted, "Would I? *Would* I!"

Ruth Elder, now making a fortune in movies and advertisements, put her career on hold to jump into the race.

When Pancho Barnes heard about the Women's Air Derby, she didn't just want to enter the race. She wanted to *win*. And she was one of the few pilots who could afford to order her own plane just for the derby.

Louise Thaden was so determined to get into the derby, she flew to the Travel Air factory in Wichita to talk to Walter Beech. Beech had given Thaden her first shot in aviation. Now her goal was to persuade him to build her a winning plane.

Amelia Earhart wanted into the derby, too. She *needed* in. She was the most famous female pilot in the world, but was she really an elite flier? No, not based on anything she'd done so far.

Since her Atlantic flight, Earhart had been flying herself from city to city, greeting crowds of admirers, writing articles, giving lectures, and struggling to keep up with mountains of fan mail. It was a great life—working in aviation and using her public voice to challenge traditional ideas about what we'd now call gender roles.

"I know many boys who should, I am sure, be making pies, and girls who are much better fitted for manual training," Earhart argued. "Too often, little attention is paid to individual talent. Instead, education goes on dividing people according to their sex."

This was a radical idea ninety years ago. In some ways, it still is.

Earhart's work was rewarding and important. Still, she couldn't shake the feeling that she needed to prove herself as a pilot, both to herself and to her rivals. The Women's Air Derby was the perfect chance to show she belonged.

Or the perfect chance to humiliate herself.

Amelia Earhart was the most famous female flier in the world. People were going to expect her to *win*.

Another top contender would be Ruth Nichols, a twenty-eight-year-old pilot from New York.

Nichols, unlike so many of her rivals in the derby, had *not* been a jump-off-the-roof kind of girl. Her father, a gifted athlete and wealthy stockbroker who'd fought alongside Teddy Roosevelt in the US Cavalry, pushed Ruth into activities that terrified her, things like competitive horse jumping and diving from the highest platforms at the pool.

It was a lot for a timid kid to handle. As she'd later say, "I spent most of my childhood with my heart in my mouth."

"Formidable opposition," Ruth Nichols said of her rivals in the race. "But I was confident that with a good plane, I could give them a run for the money."

Ruth's greatest fear: heights. She hated elevators. She suffered head-spinning vertigo in tall buildings. She'd die before riding a roller coaster. When she graduated from high school in 1919, her father took her to an air show in Atlantic City, New Jersey, and bought her a ten-minute ride in an airplane.

It was a reward for doing well in school. It was also a challenge.

Refusing to let her dad see the panic surging inside her, Ruth climbed into the two-seat plane. Her eyes slammed shut as the pilot took off. She felt the wind in her hair. She heard the hum of the wind in the wings. She opened her eyes. They were high over the city and the beach—and in an instant, everything changed. She burst out laughing.

"I was free as the air itself," she recalled of this moment. "I wasn't afraid of anything anymore. I wanted to go up and up forever."

This was not what her parents had in mind.

The way they saw the world, their daughter now had two goals. First, go to finishing school, where young women of affluent families learned how to behave in polite society. Second, find a suitable husband.

Instead, Ruth insisted on going to Wellesley College. In summers, when she was supposed to be at fancy parties, she took flying lessons. After college, she got a job as an office assistant in a bank, suffering through tedious days at a desk. On weekends, she'd slip out to the airfield.

"I came home grease-smeared but happy," she'd later say. "Mother threw up her hands in despair."

Ruth Nichols's life changed a few minutes into 1928. She was home alone, longing to escape her boring life, when the phone rang. She picked it up and heard singing and bells, a raging New Year's party.

"Happy New Year, kid!" shouted Harry Rogers, her first flight instructor. "I'm flying to Miami. Want to come along?"

"Does a fish want to swim?" she asked. "When do we start?"

Three days later, Nichols and Rogers, sharing the flying, made the first nonstop flight from New York City to Miami, covering 1,200 miles in twelve hours. Newspapers dubbed Nichols "Society's Flying Beauty" and the "Debutante Aviatrix." The owner of Fairchild Aviation offered her the dream job of promoting his company by flying a Fairchild plane around the country.

Nichols thought about crossing the Atlantic. And we know that when George Putnam was looking for a woman to make the Atlantic flight, he thought of her before he'd ever heard of Amelia Earhart. Work kept Nichols busy, though. There'd be other shots to make history.

Like the Women's Air Derby.

Nichols had hundreds of hours of flight time in all kinds of terrain and weather. She knew she could win the race. After what she'd later describe as "some high-pressure telephoning," she managed to persuade the president of Rearwin Airplanes to let her borrow its newest model.

Ruth Nichols was in.

Elinor Smith was in, too. Assuming she could get a fast plane.

When she got a call from George Putnam, asking her to come in for a chat, she hoped he was going to offer to help. True, they'd met once before, and it had gone badly.

"What is your ambition?" Putnam had asked her.

Smith was seventeen and cocky. And honest. "To take Amelia's place as the number-one woman pilot," she said.

Putnam was Amelia Earhart's publisher and manager; he hadn't seemed thrilled about Smith's answer. But now, with the Women's Air Derby coming up, he'd called her again and invited her to his office in New York City.

"You know, Elinor," Putnam began, smiling at her across his massive desk, "I'm still very interested in your future."

So far so good. She waited for more.

"I fully realize the nagging financial insecurity that plagues most pilots and would therefore like to make you a generous offer. What would you think of a guaranteed seventy-five-dollar weekly income for a two-year period—as a starting figure, that is?"

The offer sounded too good to be true. Men earned an average of twenty-nine dollars a week; the average for women was seventeen.

Putnam went on to explain that his client, Amelia Earhart, was determined to compete in the Women's Air Derby. Frankly, he was worried she'd fare poorly against top competition. As part of this deal he was offering, Smith would be Earhart's so-called "mechanic" during the race. Actually, she would fly Earhart's plane.

"You would do all the difficult cross-country flying," he clarified, "but, of course, she must *appear* to be doing it. When pictures are taken at various stopovers, you will see to it that you stand to her left, so her name will always come first in the captions. You will, of course, do no writing or public speaking for another two years at least."

He slid a stack of papers toward her. "It's all spelled out in this contract."

Elinor Smith could see exactly what was happening. Putnam saw her as a threat. He was not only trying to protect Amelia, he was trying to keep *her*, Elinor, out of the race.

Smith pushed the papers back to Putnam.

She said, "I'm afraid I have other plans."

It never would have worked, anyway. Amelia Earhart never would have let anyone else do her flying.

We know this for a fact because, while Putnam was devising his scheme, the men organizing the Women's Air Derby were having second thoughts about allowing women to fly over mountains and across deserts. Worried they'd be blamed for crashes if women were at the controls, race officials suggested that women should race with a "navigator"—a man, in other words, who would do the actual flying.

They also proposed revising the course to make it shorter and safer.

"This is just what we *don't* want," Amelia Earhart told the *New York Times*. "It is ridiculous to advertise this as an important race and then set us down at Omaha for a level flight to Cleveland. As for suggesting that we carry a man to navigate, that is still more ridiculous. If we can't fly the race and navigate our own course through the Rockies, I for one won't enter. None of us will enter unless it is going to be a real sporting contest."

That threat was enough. Amelia Earhart was the biggest name in the race, and organizers needed her in. They relented—the race would be from Santa Monica, California, to Cleveland, Ohio. Each woman would fly alone.

That settled, Earhart bought herself a Lockheed Vega, one of the fastest planes in production. A monoplane with an enclosed cockpit, the Vega was far more powerful than anything she'd ever flown. Could she learn to handle it in time for the derby?

Going into the derby, Amelia Earhart had little experience flying planes as fast as the Lockheed Vega.

Elinor Smith didn't think so.

"There was absolutely no way she could have built up enough air time in that brief period to be at ease behind the controls of the fastest heavy monoplane in the air," Smith would later say. She'd flown Vegas and described the plane's performance as "unstable, tricky near the ground." The plane was heavier than anything Earhart had flown, and it had to be flown fast to keep from stalling. "The landing speed," Smith explained, "was at least a third faster than any other plane in the race, and some of the airports along the way were little more than cow pastures."

Smith was confident *she* could handle a Vega—but she didn't have the money to buy one. Several oil companies offered to lend her one in exchange for her endorsement of their products, but the deals kept mysteriously falling through. Smith suspected Putnam was working behind the scenes, using his influence in the business world to kill the deals.

For the rest of her life, Elinor Smith would blame George Putnam for keeping her out of the race.

Louise Thaden was still in Wichita. Without a plane.

Night after night, she lay in bed, wide-awake and sweating. Sleep was impossible, and it wasn't just the sticky Kansas nights. It was already August. The Women's Air Derby was less than three weeks away.

Walter Beech liked Louise and knew she'd be a strong contender. He wanted her in the race and had agreed to have Travel Air build her a new model called the Speedwing—time permitting. The factory had several Speedwing orders ahead of hers, including racing planes for Marvel Crosson, who was sponsored by the Union Oil Company, and Pancho Barnes, who was rich enough to buy her own.

All Thaden could do was wait. She tried to stay busy, studying maps and plotting courses across the country. But mostly she hung around the hangar where the crew was building Beech's sleek new planes. The Speedwing was an open-cockpit biplane with a powerful engine and innovative "speed wings"—short, thin wings designed to minimize drag. They'd be some of the fastest planes in the race.

When Marvel Crosson flew to Wichita to check on the work, she and Louise, both expert mechanics, watched men assemble airplanes in what looked to them like slow motion.

"If you girls don't keep out of the factory," Walter Beech snapped, "we never *will* get your ships out."

The first Speedwing to roll out of the hangar belonged to Marvel Crosson.

Marvel, her brother Joe, and Louise Thaden were among a small crowd at the airfield when a factory pilot took the new plane up for a test. Everything looked great. In a speed test, the plane absolutely *screamed* over the field at a jaw-dropping 168 miles per hour.

A reporter for the *Wichita Beacon* described the look on Marvel's face as "delighted."

Louise tried to hide her discouragement. She and Marvel had met a few times at airfields. They liked and respected each other. But they couldn't both win the race.

When Marvel's plane was ready, she and Joe flew it back to California. The Speedwing's big engine and short wings made it faster than anything Marvel had flown, and less stable in the air. She wasn't worried. She had her ship and time to practice with it. She was confident of winning.

Louise, meanwhile, was sick of waiting in Wichita. She decided to go see her family. She could have driven, but where was the fun in that? Why not make a grand entrance to Bentonville, with the whole town watching?

Borrowing a plane, she flew to Oklahoma to pick up her father—he was there on business. He'd never been in a plane and eagerly climbed into the front seat for the flight to Arkansas.

"Dear Lord, let me get away with this," Louise silently prayed. "I do not ask for myself, but keep Father safe."

The flight to Bentonville was smooth and easy. When she got close, she spotted thousands of people waiting for her on a golf course. There was a marching band, and a sign with six-foot letters:

WELCOME HOME OUR LOUISE

Mr. McPhetridge turned around in his seat and pointed down, beaming. He was the man who had desperately tried to talk her out of becoming a pilot. Now she could see it in his eyes—this was the proudest moment of his life.

If only she could land without killing anyone.

She had to dive toward the crowd five times before people understood they needed to clear a strip of grass. The crowd parted, and she put the plane down on the fairway. Before she could even taxi to a stop, her mother and sister rushed up, with the rest of the town steps behind. She shook hands until the bones in her right hand ached, smiled until the muscles in her cheeks throbbed.

Later, at home, Louise told her parents and sister that she was hoping to race in the first Women's Air Derby.

Her father thought it was a grand idea.

"If you enter, honey," he said, "I know you'll win."

WHY WE FLY

There were about nine thousand licensed pilots in the United States in 1929. Fewer than one hundred of them were women. Of those, twenty of the best entered the Women's Air Derby.

Many of the competitors spent the first half of August flying the cross-country course, inspecting airfields along the way. Ruth Elder and Amelia Earhart were spotted at airfields in Texas. "Miss Crosson is absorbing every bit of knowledge that might help her win," reported the *Santa Monica Outlook*. Pancho Barnes and Ruth Nichols, the paper noted, were doing the same.

By the middle of August, pilots started arriving at Clover Field in Santa Monica, where the derby was set to start on August 18. A reporter from the local paper went from plane to plane, asking each woman the same question:

"Why do you fly?"

"Because it is my profession, my way of earning a living," Marvel Crosson said.

She told the story of building a plane with her brother in their backyard.

"Would you believe it? Neither Joe nor myself could handle an airplane, and yet we owned one. What do you think of that?"

"It is too much for me," the writer confessed.

"That's about what everybody thought." Marvel laughed. "Well, Joe and I had very definite thoughts about our ship, and in no time, both of us had learned to fly it. I've been flying ever since," she said. "I love it! I love it! I love it!"

The reporter approached Bobbi Trout. "She looks like a boy, dresses like a boy," he noted. "Her stride, hand clasp, everything about her is just Bobbi Trout, that's all."

"Why do you fly?" he asked her.

"Because I do it a lot better than I do anything else."

"How did you get into the flying game?"

"The same way I got into my father's carpenter shop when I was a kid," Trout said. Instead of playing with dolls people gave her, she sneaked into the workshop and built the dolls tables and chairs. She got spanked for it. Then did it again. "It was that same urge which prompted me to keep right on trying until I learned to fly."

Next was a pilot from Texas named Vera Dawn Walker, described by the reporter as an "irrepressible 97-pound bundle of pep and ginger."

"Why do you fly?"

"Because I want to," she said.

"I'm not kidding."

"Neither am I."

At four-foot-eleven, Walker had to sit on pillows to see out of the cockpit. Just the week before, she'd broken two ribs in a hard landing. The doctor had ordered bed rest. But here she was, chest wrapped in tape, ready to race.

The reporter approached Gladys O'Donnell—"young, pretty," he noted, "fairly bubbling with the joy of living."

"Why do you fly?"

"My goodness, what a question!" she shot back. "My reasons for flying cannot be told in a few words."

She described growing up so poor that she went to school in a dress made from flour sacks. At eighteen, she married a pilot who ran a flying school. They had two children. She lived in terror of plane crashes—until Lindbergh's Atlantic flight. "Five minutes after I heard over the radio that Lindy had landed in France, I asked my husband to teach me to fly."

Papers in her hometown of Long Beach, California, started calling her "The Flying Housewife," writing mostly about what a good cook she was and how she sewed her own clothes. But Gladys O'Donnell had a secret. She was one of the best pilots in the race, with one of the fastest planes. Soon everyone would know it.

"Why do you fly?" the writer asked Pancho Barnes.

She roared: "To keep from exploding—that's why I fly!"

Louise Thaden would have had a good answer.

"Every flight has its thrills," she once said. "The thrill of beauty, of perfection, limitless space, clouds, height, color—always there is the thrill of being so gloriously alive."

But Thaden wasn't at Clover Field. She was still stuck in Wichita.

Finally, just days before the race, she watched her gorgeous blue-and-gold Speedwing roll out of the factory. Walter Beech strode up, and they stood together, admiring the gleaming machine.

"Think you can fly this ship all right, Louise?"

"If I can't," she told him, "I'd better quit."

She loaded her luggage into the front seat, eager to take off for California.

"We'll follow you to Fort Worth," Beech said, "just to be sure everything is all right."

She didn't think that was necessary. Though it would wind up saving her life.

"Okay, Walter," she said.

He smiled. "Good luck, fella."

As Thaden well knew, every airplane was different, even when built by the same mechanics from the same plans. There was simply no way to know how a particular plane was going to handle until you got it into the air. From the first moment, Thaden loved the Speedwing's quick response to her skilled touch. "The plane flew beautifully," she'd later say. "Trim, sleek, fast."

But *something* didn't feel right. Nerves, she figured. Or the August heat.

She stopped in Tulsa, Oklahoma, for fuel and a cold Coke. Walter Beech walked up. He could see she was struggling.

"Do you feel all right?" he asked.

"Sure. Swell."

It was a lie. She was light-headed and fighting the need to throw up. But she *had* to get to the starting line. They took off for Fort Worth, Texas.

Thaden started sweating, worse than before. She held tight to the stick, but the plane wasn't responding as it should. Everything was happening in a haze. Her head was pounding, and the roar of the engine seemed to be fading. She kept herself awake by chanting the compass heading she vaguely remembered being told to follow.

"It's 180 degrees—180 degrees—Fort Worth, 180 degrees . . ."

At the Fort Worth airfield, Walter Beech scanned the darkening sky, wondering what was taking her so long.

"There she is!" someone yelled. "Against traffic!"

Beech saw Thaden's plane coming in much too fast, and with the wind at her back. Another pilot approaching the landing strip from the correct direction had to swerve to avoid a head-on crash. Thaden's wheels slammed the ground, and the plane bounced like a ball down the field. Finally rolling to a stop, she killed the engine without bothering to taxi off the runway. When she tried to climb out of the cockpit, she wobbled, passed out, and collapsed on the grass.

Beech and several other men ran up and huddled around her.

Thaden opened her eyes.

"Where the hell have you been?" Beech demanded, though he sounded more relieved than anything else.

"I don't know," she said.

"My God. This is awful!"

She managed to lift her head off the ground. She felt miles away. A bell clanged in her ears. One of the men staring down at her recognized the symptoms.

"Young lady," he said, "you've got a terrific case of carbon monoxide poisoning."

The diagnosis was correct. Mechanics pulled the plane to the side of the field and did a thorough inspection. Everything was working perfectly. Except for one thing—the brand-new Wright J-5 motor was pumping exhaust, including carbon monoxide, an odorless and deadly gas, directly into the cockpit.

Walter Beech rigged up an emergency solution, running a four-inch-wide pipe from the side of the plane into the back seat. Thaden flew the rest of the way to California with her face on the pipe, breathing fresh air carried in from outside.

"An uncomfortable arrangement," she recalled, "but certainly the lesser of two evils."

At what point did Beech begin to worry that the motors in his other new planes might have the same design flaw? That's not entirely clear.

On August 17, the day before the start of the Women's Air Derby, pilots and race officials met in a hangar at Clover Field to review the route and go over the rules.

The race would last nine days and cover 2,759 miles. The pilots would head southwest from Santa Monica, fly over the deserts and mountains of Arizona and New Mexico, race across the vast spaces of Texas, turn north and speed over the plains of Oklahoma to Kansas, turn east and cross Missouri, Illinois, and Indiana, and finally slice northeast through Ohio to the shores of Lake Erie and the finish line in Cleveland.

Official timers would record each pilot's time for each leg of the race. A total of $25,000 in prize money—more than $350,000 in today's money—would be awarded. There would be small prizes each day for the fastest times, but the main prize was for the winner of the race—the pilot with the lowest overall time from Santa Monica to Cleveland. Because so much of the route was rugged and remote, each pilot had to carry a gallon of water and food for three days and had to fly with a parachute strapped to her back at all times.

A reporter for the *Los Angeles Times* was standing outside the hangar as the meeting broke up. "They came out with serious looks," he said of the pilots.

"If the twenty of us all get to Cleveland safe and sound," Amelia Earhart told another writer, "it ought to be proof enough that women can fly, and fly as well as men."

It was hard enough just getting to the starting line. Ruth Nichols's trip west was nearly as miserable as Louise Thaden's.

A week before the race, Nichols picked up her shiny red Rearwin from the factory in Kansas.

"Give 'em heck, kid!" mechanics told her.

"Bring home the bacon!"

She planned to. But Nichols wasn't even over the state line when the motor quit cold. With seconds to react, she spotted her best option—a fenced-in pasture. She hit the ground, slammed on the brakes, and crashed through two barbed wire fences. Nichols jumped out and was amazed to find no major damage, just some ripped wing fabric.

She hitchhiked to Wichita, drove back with a mechanic, helped make some

quick repairs, and headed west across Oklahoma and Texas. Over Arizona, while she was trying to outrun a thunderstorm, an oil line burst, and the engine overheated and locked up. She made another brilliant emergency landing, swerving between clumps of sagebrush.

Nichols hadn't even told her parents she'd entered the race. She knew they wouldn't approve. Now she pictured them finding out in a newspaper headline: GIRL FLIER CRASHED IN DESERT.

Well, she wasn't about to quit now. Hiking hours to a tiny road, she flagged down a car, hitched a ride to the nearest town, and hopped a train to Los Angeles, where she persuaded the executives of Curtiss-Wright, the company that had made her motor, to fly a new one to her downed plane. She helped install the new motor, took off again, and showed up at Clover Field in oil-stained rags the night before the race.

"No time for further tests on the new motor," remembered Nichols. "No time for anything, really, but desperately needed sleep."

Two racers were still missing: a nineteen-year-old flier from Oklahoma named May Haizlip and Phoebe Omlie, the most experienced of all the entrants. If they'd been forced to land somewhere, why hadn't they at least called?

It was time to change into gowns for the prerace banquet, but many of the pilots were still waiting outside the hangar, hoping for news. Amelia Earhart found the group and told them exactly what they did *not* want to hear.

"There's an airplane down in a field just outside the airport. It's a woman pilot."

Earhart jumped into her car. Marvel Crosson and Louise Thaden insisted on tagging along. No one spoke as they sped toward a nearby farm. They could see the outlines of people standing in the dark field and the silhouette of an airplane.

A tiny Monocoupe with red and yellow stripes. Phoebe Omlie's plane. Still in one piece.

And there was Omlie, standing in the field. She was leaning on a cane, but they'd expected that—she'd broken both legs in a crack-up at an air show the year before and was still recovering. But why was she surrounded by policemen?

Omlie looked incredibly relieved to see her fellow pilots.

"I've been flying around trying to locate the airport in the dark," she told them. Unable to find it, she put down in this farmer's field. Suddenly, the police sped up, suspicious of her nighttime landing in a remote field. They accused her of being a drug smuggler.

And the sheriff *still* planned to haul Omlie to jail—until he recognized the famous Amelia Earhart. Earhart explained that she and the other pilots were in town for the Women's Air Derby.

With a grunt, the sheriff led his men back to their cars.

The news from the last missing pilot, May Haizlip, was good. She'd landed safely in Los Angeles and planned to be at Clover Field tomorrow in time for the start.

Finally, the pilots put on dresses and skirts and joined five thousand admirers at La Monica Ballroom, a massive dance palace perched dramatically over the waves at the end of the Santa Monica Pier. Only Pancho Barnes came to the party in pants, a stinking black cigar between her teeth. Also, she caused a minor stir by threatening to make a rug out of a lap dog brought along by one of the race officials. Just her idea of a gag.

It was a happy night, with dinner and speeches, a swinging orchestra and dancing. Many of the pilots had met one another at airfields over the past few years. Pilots new to the community, like Jessie Miller, had a chance to introduce themselves. As a girl in Australia, Jessie had been so tiny and slim, her friends jokingly dubbed her "Chubbie"—and the nickname stuck. She learned to fly while visiting England and shot to fame in 1928 with an epic, 159-day air journey from Great Britain to Australia. One other derby contestant was from overseas, German pilot Thea Rasche, a popular stunt flier at air shows in Europe and the United States.

Late that evening, as the party was breaking up, Rasche walked up to Louise Thaden.

"What do you think of this?" she asked.

Thaden's eyes widened. Other racers gathered around to look at the yellow slip of paper in Thea's hand. It was a telegram, sent to her from New York City. It was unsigned. The message was just three words:

WESTERN UNION TELEGRAM

Received at 1-2-25

NYC

BEWARE OF SABOTAGE.

CY223PM

STARTING LINE

"Today the eyes of the entire United States are on this little handful of women who are making air history," announced the *Santa Monica Outlook* on the morning of August 18. Race day.

The paper also included a feature called: "Pick the Winner of the Women's Air Derby: Win $10"—readers could send in their predictions for a chance to win.

There was a lot more than ten bucks at stake for the pilots. Besides the hefty prize money—and the thrill of victory—pilots were competing for endorsements from oil and plane companies, for offers to earn money demonstrating planes and giving lectures about aviation. They were competing for a chance to earn a living in the only field of work they loved.

By dawn, the pilots were at Clover Field. They checked weather reports, tested the bracing wires and control cables on their planes, polished wings, and filled fuel tanks. They slid under their ships, wiping off every smudge, every dead bug—any debris would increase drag and cost them speed.

Many Women Enter Santa Monica-Cleveland Women's Air Derby—Zep Hangar at Akron

Fans—and gamblers—tried to predict the winner of the Women's Air Derby.

The first leg of the derby would be sixty-eight miles, a relatively short hop between mountain ranges to San Bernardino. Pilots marked their routes on road maps, adding notes about landmarks to watch for. Newspaper writers started showing up, looking for some new angle to report.

"This race is going to show people that we women can fly," said racer/ movie star Ruth Elder. "It's going to be the first cross-country solo flying for me. And, oh boy, am I going to keep my eyes open! There are some tough spots on that route."

Marvel Crosson took a moment from supervising a last-second tune-up to talk about the rough terrain ahead. "It's going to take plenty of ability and navigating skill."

Bobbi Trout watched the airport crew fuel up her Golden Eagle Chief, checking to be sure the tank was completely full. She loaded a small suitcase and a jug of water into the front seat of the plane and showed reporters her good-luck charm, "a tiny, mangy, sawdust-stuffed teddy bear," as one writer described it, hanging from the compass in her cockpit.

A reporter asked Louise Thaden what she thought would be the deciding factor in the race.

"A third the breaks," she said, "a third navigation, and a third the fastest ship."

That was typical Thaden, to credit luck and the speed of the planes, factors outside the racers' control. Of course, the derby would also be a test of skill and nerves, but it wasn't her style to say so.

All the women were asked about clothing. What would they wear? What sorts of outfits would they take along? No male pilot would have to waste time with these questions, and the derby fliers didn't want to, either.

Marvel said, "I'll wear a dress under my aviator's coat and carry a toothbrush. That's all."

"Flying fast will be hard work," Gladys O'Donnell added. "This is no tea party."

By noon—two hours before the starting gun—the airplanes were lined up for takeoff. The temperature was ninety degrees and rising.

Thousands of fans roamed around Clover Field as bands played, movie stars posed for pictures, and planes buzzed overhead shooting film footage. A Goodyear blimp floated slowly down to the dusty runway, and the mayor of Santa Monica jumped out of the airship's cabin, along with his special guest—Amelia Earhart.

The pilots pushed their way through the crowds to race headquarters for a final briefing.

"It was a madhouse," Louise Thaden would later say. "Phones ringing, reporters, field officials, race officials, contestants."

Thea Rasche showed a race official the anonymous "beware of sabotage" telegram she'd gotten the night before.

"Don't worry," the man told her. "This will be taken care of."

As the pilots came out of the meeting, Pancho Barnes and Marvel Crosson tried to cut the tension by clowning around for a movie camera.

"Well, Marvel," Pancho said, giving her rival's hand an exaggerated shake, "I'm certainly going to try to win this race, but if I don't, I hope you do."

Marvel laughed. "Thanks, Pancho. May your landings all be slow and low."

They walked off-camera arm in arm.

"I don't care what you guys write about their bravery, their skill, their sportsmanship," one reporter griped to his colleagues. "What I'm gonna say is, them women don't look good in pants."

Another writer saw some of the pilots touching up makeup before being photographed. "Well," he teased, "it looks like a powder puff derby to me!"

Over the next nine days, through the derby's spectacular and tragic twists and turns, articles all over the country would refer to the race as the "Powder Puff Derby." And the racers were "Ladybirds" and "Derbyettes" and "Flying Flappers" and "Petticoat Pilots" and "Sweethearts of the Air." It was patronizing and stupid, and the women had heard it all before.

Amelia Earhart said, "We are still trying to get ourselves called just 'pilots.'"

Louise Thaden bought a hot dog and a bottle of soda and ate lunch while she walked to her plane. She was still thinking about that telegram. Who would sabotage the racers' airplanes?

There were powerful men who hated the idea of women flying, the idea of women breaking free of traditional roles. But would they go so far as to tamper with the planes? Risk the women's lives just to make them look bad?

What about rival racers or gamblers? There were rumors of heavy betting on the derby—could *that* be behind the warning?

No time to think about it now.

The racers were divided into two categories, based on the power of their planes' engines. The "light" planes were flown by Phoebe Omlie and Bobbi Trout—who were seen as most likely to win this division—along with Chubbie Miller, Thea Rasche, Claire Fahy, and Edith Foltz.

The "heavy" division was wide open—favorites included Pancho Barnes, Marvel Crosson, Louise Thaden, Amelia Earhart, and Ruth Nichols. Ruth Elder was in the hunt, too, alongside Gladys O'Donnell, Vera Dawn Walker, and six other contenders: Blanche Noyes, Margaret Perry, Neva Paris, May Haizlip, Opal Kunz, and Mary von Mach.

The heavy planes were faster and flashier—winning the heavy division was the big prize of the derby.

Pancho Barnes was so confident she invited friends to meet her in Cleveland for a victory celebration.

Amelia Earhart was not one to make predictions. She climbed into her Lockheed Vega, knowing that she had the fastest plane in the race—and that she did not have the experience to fly it safely.

Ruth Nichols had a different concern. She had a fast plane but didn't want to push her new motor too hard right out of the gate. "I would be far outclassed by faster planes at the start," she'd later say. "But at least I was in the race!"

Gladys O'Donnell kissed her kids, ages four and six, before getting into her red-and-black Waco 10 biplane.

"Win the race or bust, Gladys," her husband said.

She pulled her goggles over her eyes. "I'll do my best. See you in Cleveland."

Vera Dawn Walker's brother gave her a good-luck hug.

"Don't hug me so tight, Buddy," she said. "Remember those two ribs are still cracked."

Louise Thaden tossed away the unfinished nub of her hot dog. She climbed into her cockpit, her throat tight with nervous excitement.

From her cockpit, Marvel Crosson waved to her mother and father. Joe was working but would meet her in Cleveland—hopefully, to celebrate. Emory Bronte, Marvel's fiancé, would be there, too. He'd written her a short note, which she carried with her in the plane.

Sweetheart:
Goodbye and good luck. I know everything will be alright and that you are going to win. Will be with you every minute and waiting for you at Cleveland.

Love, Emory

"I will now give you your final instructions," a race official announced to the pilots over the loudspeakers at Clover Field.

The planes would take off one at a time, the official explained, with one minute between takeoffs, for safety. Lighter planes would take off first, with the goal of keeping the entire group reasonably close together. Each plane would be timed separately, starting at takeoff and ending when it flew over the finish line painted on the field at the end of each leg of the race. Each plane's time for each leg would be added up. Lowest overall time would win the derby. The first stop was San Bernardino.

The pilots knew all this. More than one shouted, "Let's go!"

"You will receive ten drops of the red flag," the official continued. After the starter waved his red flag ten times, he'd wave his white and red flags together—the signal to take off. "That's all," said the official. "Good luck!"

At exactly 2:00 PM Pacific time, National Air Races director Cliff Henderson fired a starting gun in Cleveland. The blast was carried live on NBC radio to the entire country and broadcast over the speakers at Clover Field.

The starter waved his flags for Phoebe Omlie. The crowd roared as Omlie's plane shot forward and climbed into the sky.

"They're off!" cried the Clover Field announcer.

One by one, the other light planes took off. Bobbi Trout's Golden Eagle was the last of the small planes to climb over the field.

"That's number one hundred, Bobbi Trout!" shouted the announcer—each plane had a number painted on its side so fans could identify it. "Everybody wave to her!"

The faster planes moved into position. Pilots waited in their cockpits, tightening seat belts, wiping sweaty hands on coveralls, looking over cockpit gauges, checking and rechecking maps they'd already memorized. Finally, the starter's flags started waving.

Marvel was first. She eased forward on the throttle, feet jammed on the brakes to keep from leaping into motion, counting the flags as they fell.

Eight, nine, ten!

The white flag fell, and Marvel burst down the field, kicking up dust. Rising over the crowd, she banked sharply and headed east.

"Second of the big ships to leave is a Travel Air, piloted by Florence Lowe Barnes!" boomed the announcer's voice through the loudspeakers at Clover Field. "She is best known to the flying fraternity as Pancho—one of the greatest fliers that ever wore pants!"

Next up was Blanche Noyes, one of the newest pilots in the race. A twenty-nine-year-old stage actor from Cleveland, Blanche had learned to fly from her husband, an airmail pilot named Dewey Noyes. "That wife of yours had better be good," a government inspector told Dewey the day of Blanche's flight test, "or I'm going to flunk her on general principles because she's a woman." She passed, making her the first woman to get a pilot's license in Ohio. That was less than a month before the derby.

Now she was in the air, racing against the biggest names in the sport.

Next it was Louise Thaden's turn.

"I'm away!" she screamed at the top of her lungs as her plane bolted forward. Weeks of pre-race jitters dissolved the moment she left the ground.

Amelia Earhart took off, then Margaret Perry.

"Next to go is Ruth Nichols," shouted the voice over the loudspeaker, "the famous pilot who, on her way to California, was brought down in the Arizona desert, put a new engine into her machine, arrived on time, and is here to put up a game fight!"

After Nichols went Opal Kunz and Neva Paris.

Ruth Elder waited her turn, feeling more alone than when she'd been lost over the wide Atlantic. "I won't say I was petrified," Elder said that evening, "but I will admit that my throat was so dry that I couldn't even force a noise out of it."

Elder finally got into the air, followed by Gladys O'Donnell.

"And last to go is Vera Dawn Walker," the announcer told the crowd. "Less than one hundred pounds of grit and determination—and there she goes! Good luck to you, Vera, too!"

Almost immediately, something went wrong. The crowd at Clover Field looked up and pointed as one of the planes turned around and headed back to Clover Field.

"Number six!" cried the announcer—Amelia Earhart. "We're trying to get the information for you as soon as possible!"

Mechanics sprinted out to meet Earhart's Vega as it landed. She pointed out an electrical short she'd noticed right after takeoff. The mechanics fixed it quickly, and she got back on the course. But she'd lost fourteen precious minutes.

Marvel Crosson raced through smooth air at about one thousand feet. Between the beating sun and the blast of engine exhaust, the temperature in Marvel's open cockpit soared to 120 degrees. But she was used to that. Flying

conditions were good—blue skies and clear views of the mountains to the north and south and the roads below.

Marvel flew with her road map open on her lap.

Seriously, a road map.

Of course, she couldn't read road signs from one thousand feet up, but she could make out landmarks like intersections, railroads, and small towns. Every few minutes, she'd hold the control stick with her knees and crane her neck to see over the side of the cockpit. Then she'd check the view she'd just seen against the road map in her lap, using a finger to trace the route she'd drawn on the map the night before.

This was how pilots navigated across the country. It was the only way to stay on course.

About halfway to San Bernardino, Marvel spotted a plane about a mile to the north. She recognized it—Pancho's Speedwing. She watched Pancho cruise past her into the lead. Turning in her seat, Marvel saw Louise Thaden coming up fast.

Not surprising. Pancho and Louise were probably the most aggressive fliers in the race, with two of the fastest planes. Marvel's strategy was a bit different. She was holding back a bit at first, disguising her ship's true power.

It was far too soon to panic.

SAN BERNARDINO

For Phoebe Omlie, it happened in the middle of physics class. One moment she was daydreaming about becoming an actress. The next moment, the only thing she wanted to do was fly.

It was 1919. Phoebe was a high school senior in St. Paul, Minnesota. She was sitting in class, thinking about her future, when sounds from outside interrupted the teacher's lecture. Students ran to the window. They knew President Woodrow Wilson was visiting town, and there he was in the street below, crowds lining the sidewalks and cheering as his car rolled slowly past.

But Phoebe Omlie was looking up.

There was another sound, and it was coming from the sky. Three army planes buzzed above the motorcade, performing climbs and rolls over the city.

A voice in Phoebe's head screamed, "That's what I want to do—this is it!"

She started flying lessons and practiced the kinds of death-defying stunts that drew crowds to air shows. At nineteen, Phoebe walked on the wings of flying planes. She danced on the wings and did handstands. She dangled under the plane from the end of a rope—then clamped the rope between her teeth and let go with her hands.

For a showstopper of her own invention, Phoebe would leap from a plane, open a parachute, drift down toward the crowd—then cut the chute free and tumble into a free fall. The audience gasped and wailed, thinking her chute had failed. At the last moment, she'd open a second parachute.

She twisted a few ankles with hard landings. Once she fell onto utility wires and got badly burned. "Don't put it in the papers," she pleaded with a reporter from her hospital bed. "I don't want my mother to worry."

Omlie went on to become an expert pilot, the first woman to earn a transport license. During the devastating Mississippi River flood of 1927, she flew over flooded farms and towns, dropping life-saving food to families stranded in trees and on rooftops. On a routine flight in October 1928, the controls of her plane locked up 250 feet above the ground. She came down nose first,

Wing-walking was just one of Pheobe Omlie's death-defying air stunts.

shattering her legs so badly doctors told her they would both have to be amputated.

Omlie kept her legs, but recovery was painfully slow. By the time of the Women's Air Derby, ten months after her crash, she still had metal braces on both legs. She needed a cane in each hand to walk.

She did not even think about skipping the race. She fully expected to be the first light plane to Cleveland. And no one passed her on the first leg. Thirty-two minutes into the flight, she saw the sign helpful residents had painted on a flat roof in twelve-foot-high letters:

SAN BERNARDINO

Omlie spotted the airfield nearby, nosed down to gain speed, and zipped over the finish line at 130 miles per hour. The moment her propeller crossed the line, an official on the ground waved his flag, and the timekeeper noted the time.

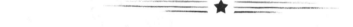

Second over the line was Bobbi Trout, who had managed to pass the other planes in the light class. Bobbi circled the airfield and landed on a narrow strip of grass between thousands of race fans and their cars—they'd driven right onto the field.

The crowd looked up and cheered as three of the heavy planes sped toward the line. Pancho Barnes was first over. Marvel Crosson crossed two seconds later, with Louise Thaden on her tail.

Race officials had sprinkled the landing strip with water to limit the dust, but with planes landing in quick succession and kicking up dirt, the air over the field turned brown and hazy. Opal Kunz couldn't see the grass and slammed down from ten feet—what pilots called a "pancake"—damaging her landing gear.

A minute later, Amelia Earhart came in fast and overshot the runway. Her plane touched down too far down the field, reported the *San Bernardino Sun*,

"causing the crowds to jump hither and yon looking for something to crawl under."

It was an embarrassing start for Amelia, and exactly what Elinor Smith had worried about—that the Vega's fast landing speed would cause Earhart problems at short airfields.

As pilots taxied off the field, enthusiastic crowds charged up and surrounded the planes, touching them, grabbing them. Children jumped onto wings, and overly excited adults actually poked the tips of umbrellas into the tight fabric covering the racers' planes, curious to see what was inside.

Fabric was easy enough to repair. The lack of crowd control was the real problem.

The pilots would soon look back on the chaos at San Bernardino and wonder. Is that where their troubles began?

Pancho Barnes jumped out of her plane and lit a cigar.

"It's some feeling to have arrived first," she told reporters and photographers as they gathered around. "Here's hoping I get to Cleveland in the same position."

Pancho's official time from Santa Monica was twenty-seven minutes and twenty-one seconds. The top of the heavy-plane standings after Day One looked like this:

RACER OVERALL TIME

Racer	Time
Pancho Barnes	27:21
Louise Thaden	27:50
Gladys O'Donnell	29:19
Marvel Crosson	29:23
Blanche Noyes	31:15
Ruth Nichols	32:50

Phoebe Omlie finished the leg in an impressive 32:15, faster than most of the more powerful planes. Bobbi Trout was in second place in the light-plane division, five minutes behind Omlie.

Amelia Earhart sat a distant eleventh place among heavy planes. Her actual flying time was good enough for third, but the fourteen-minute delay at Clover Field left her at the back of the pack. She wasn't worried, she told reporters. She could make up the lost time over the next two or three days.

Ruth Elder, in seventh place, felt the same. "There is plenty of space between here and Cleveland to allow me to catch up—if I can." Her main concern was navigation, especially in the western United States, where she'd rarely flown. "Personally, I don't know the country very well," she said. "One of the things I'm most afraid of is losing a lot of time by getting off the course."

That's exactly what happened to Chubbie Miller on Day One. The Australian pilot veered fifteen miles off course before realizing her mistake; an understandable error since she was new to the United States. The *San Bernardino Sun* cut her no slack, noting, "She could have made it about as quickly in an automobile."

Later that afternoon, away from the reporters, Marvel told Pancho that something hadn't felt right during the first flight of the race. Marvel didn't seem to think it was anything serious. They agreed she should have her plane thoroughly checked out in Phoenix, after the next day's flights.

Then it was time for the banquet.

After the strain of the first day, and all the buildup before it, the pilots just wanted to work on their planes, study their maps, and get some rest. Instead, they were driven to a hotel and given just enough time to clean up and pull crinkled evening clothes from their overnight bags. Then they were driven to another hotel and led into the ballroom for the evening banquet.

The pilots shook hands and smiled politely. Pancho Barnes and Phoebe Omlie were given prizes for fastest times of the day, and all the women were asked to say a few words to the crowd. There were musical numbers, a fancy dinner, and endless speeches by local politicians.

This would become a painful pattern over the next eight nights. Even the plate of chicken was always the same.

Marvel Crosson managed to steal a few moments with a friend of hers from high school. The friend could see that Marvel wasn't feeling very well. Marvel insisted it was nothing. She was eager to get back in the air.

It was past midnight when the pilots got back to their hotel. They finally had time to look over the route for Day Two and noticed that race officials had made a last-minute addition to the route, a quick stop in the border town of Calexico, California.

Fliers who knew the area hated the Calexico stop. The field there was too short for the bigger planes to land safely. Race officials hadn't considered this—they were just trying to satisfy as many race sponsors and fans as possible.

Pancho Barnes grabbed a pen and paper and wrote:

"We, the undersigned pilots in the Women's Air Derby, hereby declare we will go no farther than this point, San Bernardino, unless routed by or through Yuma instead of Calexico."

Marvel, who was sharing a hotel room with Pancho, signed. Pancho stomped down the hallway, banging on doors, getting signatures. Woken from their beds in Cleveland, race officials proposed a compromise: the racers would fly *over* Calexico but not land there. Then they'd stop in Yuma, Arizona, before continuing on to Phoenix.

Satisfied, the pilots finally got to bed a little after 2:00 AM.

They were back at the airfield two hours later.

"Wisps of gray fog clung in thin strips to the valley floor," Louise Thaden recalled of the early-morning scene. "Hollow-eyed, we shivered in the chill."

The pilots in San Bernardino (from left to right): Thea Rasche, Margaret Perry, Vera Dawn Walker, Neva Paris, Louise Thaden, Jessie "Chubbie" Miller, Ruth Elder, Edith Foltz.

Takeoff was set for 6:00 AM. It was safer to start early. The desert air would get hotter and more turbulent as the day wore on.

The fliers began their preflight checks—and started finding problems.

No one had guarded the planes overnight, and people had clearly been in the cockpits, touching controls, flipping switches. When Ruth Elder checked her gas tank, she was stunned to find it filled with motor oil. Motor oil, which was meant to lubricate the moving parts of the engine, would cause the engine to fail if used in place of gasoline.

How could someone working at an airport not know the difference between oil and gas, or where each went in the plane? Luckily, Ruth discovered the mistake in time to have the oil drained and replaced with gasoline.

Assuming it *was* a mistake. Chubbie Miller found oil in her gas tank, too.

The pilots talked among themselves. How could this have happened? Was the crew at the airfield incompetent? Had some of the over-enthusiastic race fans tried to help take care of the planes?

Was something else going on?

Louise Thaden wondered again about that ominous "beware of sabotage" telegram.

She chased the thought from her mind as a reporter asked about her strategy for Day Two.

"I'm going to get every last bit of speed out of this jewel," Thaden said of her plane. "Being here to race with these women is the happiest time of my life."

Back at the hotel, Bobbi Trout bolted up in bed.

"Oh, bugs! They forgot to call me!"

She looked at her watch and realized with horror that she'd overslept. She dashed downstairs and through the lobby, almost colliding with Thea

Rasche—the hotel desk had forgotten her wake-up call, too—and together they jumped into a taxi and raced to the airfield.

Bobbi climbed into her plane a few minutes before takeoff and quickly looked over her map of the day's route. She didn't think to check her fuel that morning. Before leaving the field the night before, she'd insisted on watching the crew pump gasoline into her plane until she could see it overflowing.

Later that day, she would have reason to wish she had checked.

The start of the derby was on the front page of newspapers all over the United States that morning, with articles about the race, maps of the course, and photos of the pilots, all under big headlines:

WOMEN FLIERS BEGIN AIR DERBY

YOUNG PILOTS HOP OFF IN FIRST WOMEN'S AIR DERBY

FAIR FLIERS SPEED ACROSS COUNTRY IN AIR DERBY

It was everything race organizers had hoped for. The pilots were glad to get the attention, too—they were out to prove they could fly as well as anyone. Of course, all the interest came with a risk. If something went wrong, the whole country would know it.

Starting on Day Two, the racers took off each morning in reverse order of the standings. The plane with the slowest overall time would leave first, then the next slowest, and so on. The starter's flag fell at 6:00 AM. Chubbie Miller, who'd fallen to last place with yesterday's unintentional detour, was in the air.

Louise Thaden strapped her overnight bag into her front seat. She chased a lizard from her cockpit and warmed up her engine. By the time she taxied to the starting line, the air was so filled with dust the far end of the field disappeared into a brown haze.

The sky cleared as the racers soared above San Bernardino. They flew with their road maps open, looking back and forth between routes marked in red and cockpit compasses and the landscape sliding by beneath.

Following roads to the southwest, they aimed for Mount San Jacinto, a good landmark at over 10,800 feet. Skirting the west side of the peak, they sped into the roadless desert, following a compass heading of 120 degrees and watching for the Salton Sea, a huge, shallow lake. From there it was a straight shot south to Calexico.

Visibility was excellent, and the morning air was smooth. Yesterday had basically been a warm-up. Now the race was really on.

TROUBLES BEGIN

Marvel Crosson pushed her plane harder on Day Two. Zipping past one racer after another, she was first to fly over the cheering fans at the Calexico airfield. From there she swung east, efficiently cutting over a corner of Mexico on her way to Yuma.

Behind Marvel, the trouble began.

As soon as Ruth Elder took off, black smoke started shooting from the front of her plane—remnants of oil in the gas tank, she figured. The motor was fine, but she had to circle the field while she reached for a handkerchief to wipe soot off her goggles.

The bigger issue was navigation—it just wasn't her strength. She had the map on her lap, but even on routine flights, the cockpit of an open plane like Elder's was hot, loud, windy, and bouncing up and down. She was having trouble following her route.

And that was before a burst of wind ripped the map from her hand and sent it fluttering free.

Oh well, nothing to do but follow her compass in the general direction of Yuma.

Claire Fahy's trouble was a lot more serious.

Flying in her open-cockpit biplane, Fahy was about five hundred feet above the desert when she heard an alarming *TWANG!* Her head swung toward the sound, and she saw that two of the bracing wires between her top and bottom wings had snapped and were flopping loose in the breeze.

How long before the wings collapsed? She wasn't sure. Should she bail out and use her parachute? She was too low. She had to put the plane down, *now*. By sheer luck, the Calexico airfield was coming into view.

"The fact that I was over a field surely saved my life," she told reporters after landing.

Fahy explained the unplanned stop to race officials, then ran her hands over her snapped wing wires, wondering why they would have suddenly given way in the air. Something about the severed ends of the wires didn't look natural.

She immediately began to suspect someone had tampered with her plane.

Thea Rasche was also forced down that morning. She had passed Calexico and was flying east along the Mexican border when the motor of her biplane belched, rattled, and quit. Rasche made an emergency landing at a cattle ranch.

When a mechanic came out to take a look, he first suspected she'd run out of fuel. On closer inspection, he found that the fuel line was clogged with debris he described as "rubber, fiber, and many other impurities."

Rasche had been flying for five years. She knew that dirt could work its

Claire Fahy shows reporters the severed wire that brought her plane down.

way into fuel tanks. "But I never saw gasoline that dirty," she told a reporter. "My idea is that all that dirt couldn't have been in the tank unless someone had put it there."

Of course, Rasche immediately thought of that strange telegram she'd gotten from New York. Race officials had assured her they were going to take care of it.

But had they? Why hadn't anyone been guarding the planes in San Bernardino?

★

Bobbi Trout was making great time that morning. She zoomed over Calexico ten minutes before Phoebe Omlie, snatching the overall lead. Then disaster struck.

Just six miles short of Yuma, Trout's engine made an ugly coughing sound and died.

There was no panic; she'd made plenty of landings with a dead engine. Spotting the brown soil of a farmer's field, she coasted toward it, thinking, "Must be dirt in the carburetor or something. I'll land and fix it and be on my way."

She was only a few feet over the field when she saw it had been plowed with deep furrows—and she was coming in at a right angle to the trenches. The plane's wheels caught in a deep rut, and the plane flipped over and skidded to a stop upside-down.

Bobbi undid her seat belt and slid out of the cockpit. She tumbled head-first to the soft earth, amazingly unhurt, and walked around the wreckage of her beautiful plane.

Later that day, when she was able to get mechanics out to the field, they discovered that she'd run out of gas. It made no sense. She'd watched the crew fill her tank the night before. She was an experienced endurance flier and knew how to manage fuel for long flights. She should have had plenty of gas to reach Yuma.

Amelia Earhart was coming in too fast again.

The Yuma airfield was nothing more than a 160-acre square of sand, with one small building off to the side. Race officials stood by the building,

Marvel Crosson (left) and Vera Dawn Walker surrounded by race fans in Yuma. The smiles would fade as the temperature soared that morning.

stopwatches and official forms in hand, recording times as each plane sped over the finish line.

Earhart touched down too fast and too far down the field. When she hit the brakes, trying to stop before slamming into desert scrub, the nose of her plane fell forward, and the propeller smashed into the sun-baked dirt.

After a long, quiet moment, fans were relieved to see Amelia open the top of her cabin and wave to the crowd. Whatever panic she may have been feeling was well-hidden behind her smile.

But the news from the mechanics was bad. The Vega's propeller was ruined. She'd need a replacement—or she was out of the race. Earhart ran to the airport phone, called a supplier in Los Angeles, and was told a new prop could be flown there in three hours.

"If you all will allow me that time," she explained to the other racers, "I think I can have the prop on."

The pilots voted to delay the second leg of the day. They wanted Earhart in the race, both for the sake of competition *and* because one of their main goals was to prove in a very public way that women could fly as well as men. The derby wouldn't get as much attention from the press without its most famous flier.

The hard part was the wait.

"Have you ever stood in front of an open oven on a very hot summer day?" Louise Thaden later asked, trying to describe her misery. "Yuma, Arizona, even at nine in the morning, was broiling."

The day got hotter as the sun rose higher. Pilots hid in thin shadows beneath the wings of their planes. Scorching wind blew sand in their eyes and mouths. Heat rose from the desert floor in visible waves.

"Three hours of this," Thaden recalled, "and we were on the verge of sunstroke."

Marvel Crosson looked particularly ill. But they were all suffering.

"I really thought I was going to die," Vera Dawn Walker said later. "I was never so glad to take off."

"The first plane will leave here at twelve noon," the starter announced when Amelia Earhart's plane was finally ready. "Planes will follow at two-minute intervals, instead of the customary one-minute interval, to give the dust time to settle."

He was covered in dust. Everyone was covered in dust.

Derby rules stated that at stops during the day, planes took off in the order they'd come in. Marvel, who'd flown the fastest leg from San Bernardino, was off first. Pancho left two minutes later.

Louise Thaden waited her turn, baking in her cockpit, bulky parachute strapped uncomfortably to her back, sweating streaks through the sand caked to her face. She was relieved to get into the air. At first. The smooth morning air was long gone. Thaden knew right away she was in for a rough ride to Phoenix.

It didn't seem possible, but the cockpit was even *hotter* now, so hot it was hard to breathe. Sweat glued her legs to the seat and poured from under her leather helmet. But the real problem was the turbulence. Air moves like water, in currents and waves, and drafts of hot air flowing up from the desert tossed Thaden's plane like a raft on stormy seas. The needle of her compass bounced and spun uselessly. She had to fly with two hands clamped on the stick, fighting for control.

Like all pilots, she was trained to constantly watch for an emergency-landing spot. The air was so clear she could see mountains one hundred miles away. What she could *not* see was anywhere to land. Nothing but scrub-dotted hillsides.

Dropping low in search of calmer air, she skimmed through a rock-strewn valley. The plane hit an invisible wave, and her head snapped forward and smashed into the windshield, cracking the glass of her goggles as oil from the engine sprayed her face. Images of the crumpled remains of her plane sped through her mind. Images of crawling out from the wreckage and into the blazing sun. Stranded, injured, and very far from help.

"Well, this is a race," she told herself. "You have to take a few chances."

Thaden sighed with relief when she spotted a patch of green in the distance—Phoenix.

At Phoenix's Sky Harbor airfield, a crowd of about ten thousand watched Louise Thaden's plane skim over the trees and speed across the white finish line. Pancho Barnes roared over the line a minute later. Both planes climbed, circled the field, and set down on the dirt runway.

Phoenix police officers physically held back a surge of reporters and race fans as the other planes landed in quick succession. Boy Scouts from a local troop held out cups of ice water as the pilots trudged past the cheering crowd. The women were covered with dirt and oil, soaked with sweat, visibly stressed and exhausted. They'd all fought the violent turbulence into Phoenix.

A few agreed to answer questions for the press.

Ruth Elder told of finding oil in her gas tank and losing time as smoke billowed from her motor. "I couldn't get my goggles clear to see where I was going," she said. "I must have lost ten minutes flying in circles."

Chubbie Miller described the chaos at San Bernardino the night before. "I returned to the field after dinner and found every switch and throttle on the plane—gas, ignition, primer, everything—turned on by inquisitive persons who climbed in and out of the plane at will with no one to stop them. We are very weary tonight because of the lack of sleep last night."

For the second day in a row, Pancho Barnes had flown the fastest. Her overall time for the first two days was 3:21:10, putting her sixteen minutes ahead of Louise Thaden, with Gladys O'Donnell in third, a minute back from Thaden.

"Going to have to watch that gal," Louise thought of Gladys when she saw the standings. "She can fly and evidently has a fast ship."

Amelia Earhart was hit with a fifteen-minute penalty for causing the delay in Yuma, but even with the added time, she'd flown fast enough to jump all the way to fourth place, ahead of Ruth Nichols and Ruth Elder.

Claire Fahy didn't make it to Phoenix that afternoon, nor did Thea Rasche or Bobbi Trout, but race officials had expected this; they'd heard from the downed pilots by telephone. Marvel Crosson wasn't in yet, either, which was surprising.

"Now what the hell do you suppose has happened to Marvel?" Pancho asked the other racers.

Pancho said she'd seen Crosson's plane flying low to the south of her, but that was back near Yuma. No one had seen her since.

They were all a little worried, though the silence wasn't so surprising. If Marvel was stuck somewhere in that wilderness they'd just crossed, it was going to take her a while to get word to anyone.

After a short rest, the pilots gathered with 350 guests in the ballroom of the Hotel Westward Ho for the evening banquet. As they'd do throughout the race, reporters insisted on describing the women's outfits—Ruth Elder had on a "charming beaded evening gown," and Amelia Earhart sported a "tailored suit of a medium shade of blue." Louise Thaden hadn't bothered changing out of her flying clothes. Pancho Barnes strolled in sporting pants and a men's shirt.

They ate another chicken dinner. The governor made a speech, then the city manager. Local club presidents made speeches. The publisher of the *Arizona Republican* presented prizes of $200 each to Pancho Barnes and Phoebe Omlie. Then he made a speech. Then there were toasts and dancing till midnight.

The pilots hung around, yawning, reluctant to go to bed before hearing from Marvel Crosson. Rumors swirled through the ballroom. Marvel had landed somewhere and was fine. Marvel had crashed. Marvel was wandering around the desert.

A reporter slid up to Louise Thaden and whispered a bit of news he'd just heard: "Marvel Crosson is down in the mountains."

Louise demanded more information—was she all right?

"Don't know," the man said. "Searching parties are still out."

The reporter's information was accurate.

Shortly after noon that day, near Wellton, Arizona, a six-year-old girl had seen a plane flying low over her house, coming down fast. She raced inside to tell her grandmother, who called local authorities. Four ranchers also reported seeing a low-flying plane. It disappeared from view, they said, into a thicket of cottonwood trees in the dry basin of the Gila River.

The plane fit the description of Marvel Crosson's Speedwing.

A search party set out from Wellton, but it was dark by the time they reached the remote spot the witnesses had described. They found no sign of Marvel or her plane.

Back at the Westward Ho, it was another night with little sleep for the pilots.

Amelia Earhart and Chubbie Miller, who shared a room, sat up talking about how unfair it was that the public treated airplane accidents differently depending on whether the pilot was a man or a woman. When a man crashed, it was all part of the job, part of the adventure and romance of aviation. When a woman crashed, it was an intolerable calamity. That attitude, they agreed, was going to have to change.

Louise Thaden, who bunked with Blanche Noyes throughout the race, had agreed to write updates along the route for the *Wichita Eagle*. Now, after midnight, she finally had a moment to get down a few thoughts.

"We're all as tired as dogs," she wrote. "We're having plenty of entertainment, which we don't like so much, and prizes, which we do appreciate."

She reported that she clearly had one of the fastest planes in the race, along with Pancho Barnes, Gladys O'Donnell, and Amelia Earhart. And Marvel Crosson, of course. She refused to speculate about what might have happened to Marvel.

"We are all confident of placing in the money," Thaden wrote. "Now, if people will only let us rest, we'll be all right the rest of the way."

MARVEL

The racers read the local newspapers over breakfast in the hotel coffee shop. What little news there was of Marvel Crosson was not reassuring.

"Discouraged searching parties straggled back into Wellton late Monday night," reported the *Albuquerque Journal*, "with no reports of Marvel Crosson, San Diego woman flyer, believed to have fallen in the mountains twelve miles north of here." The searchers would head out again that morning.

Other articles mentioned rumors that the race was going to be canceled. But race officials had said nothing about canceling, and the women were determined to go on. No matter what.

The pilots were driven to the airport. They checked weather reports and worked with mechanics on their preflight checks. A large crowd watched quietly, with none of the excitement of the day before. The mood at the field was tense, wrote one reporter, "filled with foreboding."

The route for Day Three was simple and relatively short, 210 miles southeast to Douglas, Arizona, a small town on the border with Mexico.

Engines started up. Pilots taxied to the starting line and waited their turn to take off.

Claire Fahy stood in front of a group of reporters in Los Angeles that morning. Out of the race and furious, she held up the severed wires from her plane.

"I am convinced the wires had been tampered with," Fahy charged. "They were snapped as squarely as if they had been cut by pliers." She'd shown them to mechanics, she explained, and they told her they'd never seen wires break like that before.

Claire's husband, Herbert, a record-setting test pilot, stood beside his wife.

"The wires show evidence of being burned with acid," Herbert said. "I am convinced that there is something rotten in this race. I'll do everything in my power to have it called off."

In San Bernardino, an alarmed L. W. Ayers, who'd been in charge of the race in that city, conceded that crowds *had* gotten to the planes the first night of the race. "Of course, tampering with the planes could possibly have happened," he told newspapers, "but it is highly improbable."

Deputy District Attorney C. O. Thompson seemed to take the threat seriously. He immediately opened an investigation into the possibility of sabotage, calling for every member of the San Bernardino airport crew to report to his office within twenty-four hours.

Bobbi Trout was still stuck in Yuma.

Her plane was towed into town, where mechanics told her it would take three days to rebuild the engine and fix the broken wooden ribs in the wings. Asked by the local paper for a comment, Trout said that the empty gas tank that had forced her down "told a very suspicious story." She'd watched her tank being filled with 24.5 gallons, enough for three hours. She'd run out of gas after just an hour and twenty-five minutes.

"She declared without reservation," reported the Yuma *Morning Sun*, "that she thinks her tank was drained."

Years later, Trout would add another disturbing detail. "I was told by several people that they saw men out around our planes that night," she said. "Now, who they were I don't know. It might have been some men who just didn't want to see women taking their place in the air."

Louise Thaden navigated across the desert from one mountain peak to the next. Spotting Tucson, she followed roads through mountain passes to the old mining town of Tombstone, flying near enough to the slopes to see abandoned holes dug into the sides of mountains.

Continuing toward the Mexican border, she watched for smoke—Douglas, racers had been told, would be covered in smoke from the town's metal smelters. It was the only sure way to find the tiny place from the air.

Amelia Earhart followed the same route, with a quick detour to the tiny town of Casa Grande. A year before, while traveling the country giving lectures, she'd been flying over the area when she ran out of fuel and made an emergency landing on the wide dirt street in the middle of town. "I am afraid I broke speed ordinances," she admitted. Everyone had come out to greet her. And now they were out again, cheering as Earhart's Vega zipped low over the same street, saluting the town before continuing on toward Tucson.

Pancho Barnes was off course, too. But not on purpose.

Following railroad tracks toward Douglas, she began to wonder why she hadn't spotted the town or its smoke. Visibility was perfect, but there was nothing in sight but cactus plants and sand. It didn't look right.

Spotting a ranch house, Pancho put her plane down on a patch of brown grass. Men walked up, waving and smiling.

"Hola! Hola!" they shouted.

"Where am I?" Pancho asked.

One of the men pointed to the ground and said, "Mexico."

Pancho had sudden visions of local authorities showing up, asking questions, searching her plane. She wasn't smuggling liquor at the moment—but by the time they realized it, she'd have lost hours.

Kicking up dust as her plane shot forward, Pancho barely cleared a row of trees, climbed into the sky, and sped north.

The search party found Marvel Crosson that morning.

Two deputy sheriffs from Wellton led a team of men and horses through the rugged terrain along the dry Gila River. Baking in the sun, scrambling through thorny brush, they followed witness accounts into a gully lined with cottonwood trees.

It was there. The plane was there.

It looked as if it had hit the earth nose first and crumpled. Pieces of wreckage were scattered over one hundred yards of rocky ground. The searchers found a piece of the instrument panel with the cracked cockpit clock. It had stopped at 12:16. They found a purse and a log book. They were Marvel's. They checked the cockpit. It was empty.

The men stood in the streambed, looking around. On the sloped side of the gully was a human figure, a twisted form tangled in the silk of a half-open parachute. The men went over for a closer look.

It was Marvel Crosson. She was dead, killed on impact. Her shattered watch had stopped at 12:16 and 30 seconds.

The search crew wrapped Marvel in her parachute. They carried her body out of the ravine, took her on horseback to the nearest road, and put her in an ambulance for the ride to Yuma.

A few months before the race, Marvel Crosson had written a magazine

article called "How I Learned to Fly." It was a love letter to aviation, with all her favorite stories: building a plane with Joe, causing a chicken-feather blizzard when they tested the motor, becoming a pilot, happily sacrificing everything that didn't get her into the air. By eerie coincidence, the article was published the day she was found dead, at the age of twenty-nine.

"Women can do men's work in the air, and do it as well if not better," Marvel had written in the article's very last lines. "I have given up my life to prove that women are the best pilots in the world."

Louise Thaden was first into Douglas. As soon as she landed, she asked about Marvel. She was told that the body had just been found.

Reporters hung back for once, watching the pilots land, watching them react to the news. "Mrs. Thaden and Mrs. O'Donnell, close friends of the dead flyer, burst into tears," wrote the *Los Angeles Times*.

The crowd of fans at the airport looked on in dazed silence.

Joe Crosson got the news in Cleveland, where he was waiting to meet his sister at the finish line. Reeling with grief, Joe had only one clear thought—he needed to be with his parents. He jumped into a friend's plane and took off. He never even asked permission to borrow the plane.

Emory Bronte, who was also in Cleveland, left for Yuma on the grim mission of picking up Marvel's body and taking it home to San Diego.

A government inspector named J. G. Null left Los Angeles for Yuma to investigate the crash. But long before there were any official reports, people began to speculate—and place blame. One reporter, reading that Marvel was found tangled in her partly open parachute, claimed she must have foolishly "neglected" to open the chute after jumping from her cockpit.

In Los Angeles, Claire Fahy reminded everyone of the severed wires that had forced her out of the race. "Marvel Crosson's death," she said, "may have been caused by similar tampering."

L. W. Ayers, the race official in San Bernardino, had a different theory. "I am positive that this was due to engine trouble, which forced her down in the wild, rugged country."

No, not possible, insisted officials of the Wright Aeronautical Corporation, which had built the motor. Wright mechanics had tuned up and tested Marvel's motor at Clover Field right before the derby began.

Interviewed at the Travel Air factory in Wichita, Walter Beech called Marvel one of the most talented pilots he'd ever seen, man or woman. He said, "I will never believe that Marvel Crosson, through negligence or incompetence, was responsible for the crash."

What *had* caused the crash? Beech declined to guess.

But, tellingly, after the reporters left, Beech ordered factory mechanics to catch up with derby racers in Texas. They were instructed to check the Travel Air planes still in the race for carbon monoxide emissions.

It was a terrible night for the pilots. They sat up together in their hotel, talking about Marvel, wondering what had caused the crash.

Pancho Barnes suspected sabotage. She didn't scare easily. She was scared now.

Louise Thaden suspected carbon monoxide poisoning. That would explain why Marvel had looked so ill in Yuma, and how such an experienced pilot had lost control of her plane.

When she finally got back to her room, Louise had to summon the will to write her nightly article for the *Wichita Eagle*. "Words cannot express the sorrow we all feel tonight in learning of Marvel Crosson's death," she told readers. "If I should be so fortunate as to win first place, I will have the trophy cup engraved with her name and send it to her people."

The pilots trusted one another, Louise wrote, and were determined to go on. They all agreed, it's what Marvel would have wanted.

After another short and fitful night's sleep, Louise woke with a pounding headache, tormented by doubts and questions.

Was the race really worth it? Was it better to stop now?

Amelia Earhart was already up. As if reading Thaden's mind—and maybe wavering herself—Earhart knocked on Thaden's door. They talked briefly, reminding each other that this race was bigger than any one of them. It was about smashing limits on what women could do in aviation—and beyond.

"Marvel is cheering each one of us on," Amelia said. "You mustn't be discouraged."

Louise knew it was true. She'd written the words herself just hours before. But still, she needed to hear it.

She looked on, grateful and deeply impressed, as Amelia made her way down the hotel hallway, knocking on doors, talking to each of the pilots, encouraging them to get ready for another day of flying.

CRITICS ATTACK

WOMEN HAVE CONCLUSIVELY PROVEN THEY CANNOT FLY

AIRPLANE RACES TOO HAZARDOUS AN ADVENTURE FOR WOMEN PILOTS

WOMEN'S DERBY SHOULD BE TERMINATED

Those were just a few of the headlines in the morning's newspapers. Marvel's crash was the "I told you so" moment race critics had been waiting for.

"Air racing for women should be discouraged as a far too hazardous adventure," the *New York American* declared. "This should be the last contest of its kind."

"Such races are all right for grown, active, able-bodied men," said the mayor of El Paso, Texas, an upcoming stop on the derby, "but they are too much for women."

The *Knoxville Journal* lamented Marvel's death, saying "youth and charm like hers seems a sacrifice too great for any honors or prizes that could be gained."

All of this put enormous pressure on the officials of the National Air Races in Cleveland. They stood firm.

"The derby will go on," announced race chairman Floyd Logan. "We have no thought of halting it." The cause of Marvel's crash was being investigated, Logan said. "In addition, claims that planes of several entrants had been tampered with are under investigation."

Cliff Henderson, the National Air Races director, contacted officials at every upcoming stop on the derby route to pass on the order that all planes be carefully guarded, from the moment they landed until the time they took off.

He also sent a message directly to the racers: "Fly with all precaution, and consider winning secondary to finishing at Cleveland."

The pilots were grateful to Henderson for not caving in to demands that the race be canceled. But once they turned their attention to Day Four of the derby, they tossed aside his advice about flying scared. That was no way to win a race.

"The only thing I worried about," Louise Thaden later said, "was whether some sort of mechanical trouble would force me to drop behind."

As the pilots arrived at the Douglas airfield that morning, newspaper reporters saw strain on the women's faces. They saw exhaustion.

And they saw a new level of determination.

"It is now all the more necessary that we keep flying," Amelia Earhart told reporters. "We all feel terrible about Marvel's death, but we know now that we have to finish."

Pancho Barnes, who'd fallen from first to fourth place after her Mexican detour, grabbed a brush and painted "Mexico or Bust" on the side of her plane. The joke seemed to lift her spirits. She boldly predicted she'd retake the lead within the next two days.

Going into Day Four of the derby, Louise Thaden was in first place. Gladys O'Donnell and Amelia Earhart held second and third, followed by Pancho Barnes and Ruth Nichols.

On the morning flight from Douglas to Columbus, New Mexico, Earhart flew aggressively *over* mountain peaks rather than taking the safer route around them. After a quick stop in Columbus, the racers sped east toward Texas. Earhart picked up the Rio Grande and followed the river into El Paso for the second of the day's four scheduled stops. In the two hundred miles from Douglas, she gained an amazing twenty minutes on Louise Thaden.

Pancho Barnes flew even faster, gaining *thirty* minutes on Thaden. If Amelia and Pancho could fly mistake-free, they were clearly going to compete for the win. So would Ruth Nichols. As planned, she was pushing her new motor harder and harder each flight. She was now just seconds behind Pancho and moving up fast.

Louise Thaden and Gladys O'Donnell with helmet hair and unpowdered noses on proud display.

As the pilots landed in El Paso, excited race fans burst through the line of city police and soldiers from nearby Fort Bliss, climbing all over the planes. Movie star Ruth Elder was the first one surrounded. Elder and the other racers sat in their cockpits, gulping cold water and signing autographs. A newspaper artist shoved through the crowd with his drawing pad, hoping to sketch a few of the women.

"Gladys O'Donnell didn't bother to powder her nose," the artist complained. "Louise Thaden wouldn't even comb her hair."

★

Back in San Bernardino, Deputy District Attorney C. O. Thompson spent the day questioning airport mechanics, security guards, and race officials.

The Yuma *Morning Sun* printed a rumor from New York City "that a powerful gambling ring was seeking to make the race a 'sure thing.'" Could this be related to Thea Rasche's "beware of sabotage" telegram from New York? The newspaper provided no additional details.

In Yuma, J. G. Null, the government investigator, examined the wreckage of Marvel Crosson's plane. He found nothing to indicate that the motor, or any other component of the plane, had failed before the crash. It looked as if Marvel had vomited over the side of the plane before crashing. Null's theory was that she must have become sick from the intense desert heat and lost control of her plane. Why was her parachute partly opened? Null guessed that she must have panicked and jumped out of the plane at the last second.

Pete Hill, one of the Travel Air mechanics sent by Walter Beech, did not agree. After inspecting and modifying the other Travel Air planes in the race, Hill was convinced Marvel had suffered from carbon monoxide poisoning. He made no statements to the press, but, privately, he was convinced that she was too good a pilot for any other explanation to make sense. Inhaling carbon monoxide causes dizziness, blurry vision, nausea or vomiting, even loss of consciousness—more than enough to explain the crash. As for the partly open parachute, the logical explanation was that it simply burst open when the plane hit the ground.

We'll never know for sure. The coroner in Wellton briefly inspected Marvel's remains but did not perform an autopsy or test her blood for carbon monoxide. At the coroner's inquest—a public hearing to investigate the cause of an unexplained death—the jury's ruling was simply "accidental death."

The wind at the El Paso airfield was picking up, swirling across the landing strip, filling the sky with dust. The plan was for the race to continue three hundred additional miles to Midland that afternoon, but as the skies in the east darkened with storm clouds, race officials and pilots huddled to discuss a possible delay.

Ruth Elder said what was on everyone's mind. "If we agree to go ahead, and one of us get hurt or killed, the rest will never forgive ourselves."

Pancho Barnes, of all people, wanted to play it safe. Clearly still thinking of her friend Marvel, Pancho offered very un-Pancho-like advice: "It is much better to be one of the oldest, than one of the bravest who have passed on."

The pilots voted to stay in El Paso. And since the racers weren't scheduled to spend the night there, there was no banquet to attend. Instead, many of the women hopped on a bus and crossed the border to Juárez, Mexico, where they enjoyed a delicious dinner with no overcooked chicken, no speeches—and no Prohibition.

"Most of the flyers refused to indulge in liquors," noted the *El Paso Evening Post*, "though a few sipped sparingly of special fizzes."

That may have been putting it a bit too politely. According to other accounts, Pancho Barnes, on a dare, chugged a pitcher of beer. Louise Thaden bought a jug of her favorite cocktail—vodka and orange soda—and brought it back for the mechanics at the airfield.

Back in her hotel room early for the first time since the race began, Thaden had time to wash her hair and clean her fingernails before sitting down to study maps and write her nightly article.

"The strain of competition, daily flying and constant planning, and the worry of preparation for each day's flight, is beginning to tell on most of the girls," she wrote. The top five racers were within thirty minutes of each other, and it was anybody's game. "All I know is that I'm still out in front and being pushed hard to stay there. I'm keeping that motor wide open from now on, and I hope it stays with me."

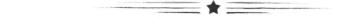

The next day's newspapers ramped up the volume on calls for the derby to be canceled.

"We admire, after a fashion, the women who are taking part in the transcontinental race," wrote an Indiana paper, "but instinctively we know that they are handicapped by their sex and that it would be better if they were not to enact a role so strenuous."

The loudest critic of all was an Oklahoma oil tycoon named Erle Halliburton. Since Marvel's crash, he'd been hounding race officials and newspapers, demanding an end to the race. "Women have been dependent on men for guidance for so long," Halliburton proclaimed, "that when they are put on their own resources they are handicapped."

He wasn't done.

"The death of Marvel Crosson, one of the best women pilots today, was needless. If it hadn't been for her fear and confusion regarding the course, she would have been leading now."

This quote especially disgusted the racers. Aside from being wrong on the facts, Halliburton was entirely missing the point of everything Marvel had lived for. Using her name to try to get the race canceled, to keep women out of the sky—it was a kind of blasphemy.

"We women pilots were blazing a new trail," Louise Thaden would later explain. "To us, the successful completion of the derby was of more import than life or death."

The women were going to finish this race. And they were not going to allow ignorance or fear to ruin the experience. The day before, reporters had seen quiet conviction on the women's faces. On Day Five, they saw eagerness, excitement, faces lit by the love of flying.

Ruth Elder blew a kiss to her adoring fans from the cockpit of her green-winged Swallow. Gunning the engine, she burst forward and climbed, shading her eyes with one hand as she sped east toward the rising sun.

To make up for the delay in El Paso, the plan for Day Five was to fly six hundred miles to Fort Worth, with stops along the way in Pecos, Midland, and Abilene. This would be the toughest day of the derby. It would go a long way toward determining the winner.

ACROSS TEXAS

At the start of Day Five in El Paso, five pilots had a serious chance to win the heavy-plane division of the Women's Air Derby.

RACER OVERALL TIME

Louise Thaden.. 6:48:31
Gladys O'Donnell 7:01:08
Amelia Earhart 7:19:47
Pancho Barnes 7:26:34
Ruth Nichols.. 7:26:36

Louise Thaden's relentless attention to detail was paying off so far. Gladys O'Donnell, little known before the race, was not going away. Amelia Earhart was gaining confidence in the cockpit of her Vega. Pancho Barnes knew she'd be winning but for some shaky navigation. Ruth Nichols, exactly as planned, was cautiously moving up the standings.

With the top racers packed so closely, any mechanical mishap, any navigational mistake, any loss of focus would shake up the standings.

Pancho Barnes saw Day Five as her day. With six hundred miles to fly in four legs, she was going to fly her race, fearless and aggressive. She fully expected to catch Louise Thaden somewhere over Texas.

Day Five was not her day.

As soon as she took off, Pancho's motor began misfiring. Staring at a steep climb toward—and hopefully over—the peaks of the Guadalupe Mountains, she knew she had to turn back. Mechanics in El Paso rushed the plane into a hangar and quickly patched a leaky gas line.

"You can't get mad over things like that," Pancho told reporters while the repair was being made. It was a routine problem and did not look suspicious. Pointing to a handcar squeaking down railroad tracks near the field, she joked, "Next time, I'll try and run one of those. I might have better luck with it."

Alone with the mechanics in the hangar, she hadn't been quite so calm.

"I won't tell what she said," Pancho's mechanic told newspapers after she'd left. "I'm too good a friend of hers."

Blanche Noyes started the day in seventh place among the big planes. It was a respectable showing for the former actress from Ohio, considering she'd passed her flight test less than a month before the derby.

Still, no one was paying too much attention to Blanche Noyes. Until her plane caught on fire. In the air.

Blanche was three thousand feet over the Texas desert when she smelled smoke. The smell was getting stronger and stronger. The unmistakable smell of burning wood started snaking into the cockpit. Fire in the air—in a plane made of wood—was a pilot's absolute worst nightmare. And *something* was obviously on fire, but she couldn't see any flames. Leaning over the side of the plane, she looked for a place to land. The ground was covered with mesquite trees.

Was she going to have to jump? She had a parachute but had never used one, and she had no confidence she'd survive the drop. Besides, she wasn't ready to give up on her plane—or the race.

"Blanche, forget about jumping," she said aloud. "You're going to land at Cleveland Airport in this plane."

She remembered something her husband had told her when she was learning to fly: "If you ever have a fire in your ship, remember to keep it out of your face! Side-slip!"

Slowing to just above a stall, she shoved the stick left and

Blanche Noyes starts her Travel Air, named *Miss Cleveland* for her hometown.

pushed the right rudder. The plane slid almost sideways through the air, losing altitude quickly without gaining speed. Knowing flames could reach the gas tank and blow her up at any moment, Blanche aimed for a flat patch of desert and straightened out at the last moment. Mesquite branches ripped her wings and cracked the left side of her landing gear as the plane touched down and jerked to a stop.

She lunged for the fire extinguisher attached to the cockpit floor. It wouldn't come out. She pulled again. Still stuck. She yanked with such force that the entire extinguisher case came free, along with the screws that had fastened it to the floor.

Jumping to the ground, she aimed the extinguisher at the flames she could now see shooting through the door of the luggage compartment on the side of her plane.

The thing didn't work.

She tossed it aside and ripped the compartment open and threw out her burning bag, beating the flames in the plane dead with her bare hands.

When it was all over, she stood in the desert beside her damaged plane. Her scorched hands started to throb. But the main thought in her head was: "I need to get on to Pecos. The clock is running."

Ruth Nichols flew first into Pecos, with Gladys O'Donnell seconds behind. Both had pulled even closer to Louise Thaden on the first leg of this long day.

After Thaden landed, Pancho's plane swooped toward the finish line—once again, Pancho had made up for lost time by flying faster than anyone.

But it was going to be a tight landing.

As at other stops along the course, thousands of people had driven to the field and parked their cars along either side of the landing strip, leaving a narrow runway for the planes to navigate. Fans watched from beside their cars, sometimes *in* their cars, inching forward with excitement as the planes came in.

Now, with Pancho Barnes coming in fast, the front end of one Chevrolet stuck particularly far out into her path. And there was no way Pancho could know it was there. With the plane's nose held high for landing, as it had to be, a pilot simply could not see directly in front of her. As Pancho touched down, her right wings slammed into the parked car. The wings snapped, and the plane spun to a stop in a cloud of dust.

Pancho jumped out, roaring with fury at the idiotic driver. The man sped away.

As mechanics were pulling Pancho's crumpled ship off the landing strip, the crowd looked up and pointed at another plane approaching the field. It was Blanche Noyes, coming down with torn wing fabric flapping, with a left-side wheel dangling like a broken limb.

"It's going to crack up!" Louise Thaden shouted, leaping from her cockpit. "Get fire extinguishers! Call an ambulance!"

Race fans and reporters backed out of the way as Blanche Noyes set her plane down expertly on its right wheel. As the plane slowed, the landing gear on the left side hit the ground and snapped. The plane swung in a loop and stopped.

The crowd gave a huge cheer for the nimble flying.

Louise Thaden ran onto the landing strip, shouting, "Are you all right?"

Blanche didn't answer. Her face was coated with soot. She lifted her hands. They were trembling and badly burned.

Blanche got out of her plane. The other racers gathered to hear the story of her fire and emergency landing. They figured that someone at the El Paso airfield that morning—a fan? a mechanic?—*someone* must have dropped a still-smoldering cigarette butt onto her bag before she loaded her luggage.

A careless mistake? Probably. But there was no way to know for sure.

"How in the world did you manage to get the ship into the air again?" Louise Thaden asked.

"I don't know." Tears slipped down Blanche's sooty cheeks. She started to sob.

Louise had been there. A crisis like that pumped a pilot full of fear. The poison had to come out, one way or another. "One of the big differences in reaction between women and men pilots," she later said, "is that women sometimes cry, and men usually go out and get drunk."

Recalling Erle Halliburton's "Women have been dependent on men for guidance for so long" line, the *Wichita Beacon* got off a zinger. "It is doubtful whether Mr. Halliburton could have set his plane down in the mesquite brush, taken it off on one wheel, and landed it on one wheel without tipping a wing, as Blanche Noyes did."

The racers still had four hundred miles to go before the day was done.

Ruth Nichols left Pecos first, followed a minute later by Gladys O'Donnell. Blanche Noyes got her landing gear welded together, covered the rips in her wing fabric with thick tape, and stayed in the race.

Pancho Barnes watched mechanics tow her plane into a hangar. Pancho was desperate to get back in the air, but her wings needed extensive repairs.

The pilots sped northeast over grassy plains, ranches, and oil wells. It was here that Louise Thaden made a costly mistake, following the wrong set of railroad tracks. "I figured to cut a few corners and gain about five minutes," she explained. "We were running so close together in the heavy division, five minutes was a lot of time. No sooner said than done, and I became gloriously lost."

Ruth Nichols was first into Midland, inching closer and closer to the front. Amelia Earhart covered the distance from El Paso so quickly that newspapers reported she'd seized the overall lead:

RACER OVERALL TIME

Amelia Earhart 9:48:17
Gladys O'Donnell 9:58:52
Ruth Nichols.. 10:00:36
Louise Thaden 10:05:19

Papers around the country rushed to press with the stunning turn of events: AMELIA EARHART TAKES DERBY LEAD.

The air got rougher as the day got hotter. After a quick lunch, the racers took off for the 150-mile flight to Abilene. This is when Chubbie Miller, the Australian pilot, flew into a tornado.

Technically, it was only the second-most-frightening crisis she'd ever had in the air.

The first had come a little over a year before, during her history-making flight from England to Australia with her friend and copilot, Bill Lancaster. At a stop in a field in what's now Myanmar, a woman took Chubbie aside to offer some advice.

"Don't forget: before you leave, have a good look inside the plane for snakes." Watch especially, she warned, for a small brown snake called a krait, which can kill with one bite. "Your machine has been sitting out in the middle of that field for some time, and all these swamps are infested with snakes."

Chubbie Miller at the start of her record-breaking trip from England to Australia.

Chubbie thought the woman was just toying with her. She and Bill got in their plane and took off with Bill at the controls. Twenty minutes later, as they flew over thick rain forest, the plane suddenly tilted and bounced.

"What's the matter!" Chubbie screamed, turning in her seat.

Bill was terrified. He pointed down and cried, "Snake!"

Guess I should have checked, Chubbie thought.

Bill stamped his boots in a crazy sitting dance, and the plane swerved and dipped toward the treetops. The snake wriggled forward into Chubbie's cockpit. Three feet long, dark brown with white bands—the venomous krait.

Pulling her feet from the floor, Chubbie yanked the control stick out of its socket and slammed it down over and over, hitting the snake, missing it, bashing it again. When it lay still, she lifted it with shaking hands and flung it over the side of the plane.

Now, 1,500 feet over west Texas, she flew into what she would later describe as "a miniature twister."

The swirling air flipped her plane upside-down and tossed her into a downward spin. Chubbie fought the controls, losing altitude, spinning and falling, watching the ground coming up fast, knowing she was too low to use her parachute. Fighting all the way down, she broke free of the twister and pulled out of the dive with a few seconds to spare.

Then she continued on to Abilene.

In San Bernardino, Deputy District Attorney C. O. Thompson announced that he had concluded his investigation into charges of sabotage at the airfield.

Though "investigation" may be too strong a word for an inquiry that lasted barely twenty-four hours.

"We have not been able to find a single instance of sabotage," Thompson told the press. "No suspicious characters were seen on the field, nor was anyone seen tampering with the planes."

That was not correct. As Bobbi Trout and others recalled, unidentified people *had* been seen near the racers' planes that first night. But no one was coming forward with specific information. If anyone *had* tampered with the planes—or knew anything about it—they either lied to Thompson or didn't show up to be interviewed.

Would a few days of detective work have uncovered important clues? We'll never know.

The matter was officially dropped that afternoon.

At Kinsolving Field in Abilene, Texas, a blazing sun beat down on five thousand race fans. It was a much larger turnout, noted the local paper, than when a men's cross-country derby had come through a year before.

Vendors pushed carts through the crowd, selling cold soda for a nickel. Newsboys waved papers, shouting:

"All the latest news about the air race!"

"Names of the pilots and numbers of the planes!"

A race official with a megaphone called updates to the crowd as fliers crossed the finish line. Amelia Earhart was first into Abilene. Reporters and photographers raced out to her plane. Mouth parched and squinting in the blinding light, Earhart patiently posed for photos.

"Tired? Rather," she confessed.

It was a day of brief quotes, mostly about exhaustion, heat, and thirst. Ruth Nichols came in next, looking, noted the *Abilene Morning News*, "very tired."

Third in was Gladys O'Donnell's red-and-black Waco. A reporter asked Gladys how she was feeling.

"Awful hot."

Louise Thaden landed, posed for a photo, and begged for a drink. "Anything," she said, "just so it's wet and cold."

Race rules required each plane to carry a gallon of water. The pilots had water in their planes—but never within reach, because there was nowhere in the tight cockpits to safely stash the jugs.

Ruth Elder taxied to a stop, managing a friendly wave to the crowd.

"Boy howdy!" chirped one reporter. "That was a million-dollar smile she gave me!"

The man with the megaphone shouted: "Yonder comes Vera!"

Abilene native Vera Dawn Walker got the biggest ovation of all. Her father was so excited he ran up to her plane while the propeller was still spinning—and would have been killed if an alert fan hadn't yanked him back. Vera shut down the motor and, cracked ribs and all, jumped into her father's arms.

"I won't win, because there are too many faster ships in the race," she told reporters. "But I'll get there. The big thing is to get to Cleveland."

Margaret Perry was the last one in. Perry was flying a fast Spartan biplane but had been slowed from the start by a fever. She kept racing, trying to ignore the fact that she was feeling worse and worse every day. In Abilene, she was too sick to continue. Reluctantly, Perry agreed to spend the night at a hotel. She planned to catch up with the group the next morning.

With guards standing watch over the planes, the pilots took a quick break under the shade of a tent. "There'll be no sabotage here," the airport manager announced. "We can promise them that!"

The last leg of the brutal day was 150 miles east to Fort Worth.

Digging deep for her last reserves of focus and energy, Louise Thaden flew low and fast over the plains, zipping past fast-moving cars and trains, past Gladys O'Donnell and Amelia Earhart.

"At Fort Worth," Thaden fondly recalled, "I oozed into first position."

As the racers landed, police officers stretched a rope between the field and the crowd of twenty thousand. Nice idea, but it didn't hold—not when the fans saw Amelia's Vega descending toward the runway.

"The surging throng broke the police lines," the *Fort Worth Star-Telegram* reported. "They crowded around the ship for a glimpse of the noted transatlantic aviator."

All the planes were quickly surrounded. Exhausted and oil-splattered, temporarily deafened from spending all day behind roaring motors, arms weak from wrestling with their controls, the pilots signed scraps of paper, pages of books, the backs of envelopes. For three hours.

And still the day would not end.

The racers were driven to a ranch on Lake Worth for the evening banquet. In a crowd of women in gowns and men in cowboy hats, the derby fliers were easy to spot. The fliers' faces were mostly tan or burned, with goggle-shaped pale patches around their eyes and pale stripes down their cheeks where helmet straps had covered their skin.

They looked, some remarked, like well-dressed raccoons.

The banquet's host presented a huge cowboy hat to Amelia Earhart. She graciously accepted the gift on behalf of all the pilots. Then came a special surprise: Two songwriters had been inspired to compose an anthem for the derby. A band began playing, and a woman at a microphone burst into song:

> *Hear the motor's steady hum,*
> *Here those flying beauties come,*
> *They're the sweethearts of the air.*
> *With their brightly laughing eyes,*
> *As they ride uncharted skies,*
> *They're the fairest of the fair . . .*

At least this was Texas—beef country. A big steak was something to look forward to.

Dinner was chicken.

"That's all we've been fed at every stop," Gladys O'Donnell moaned. "I refuse to eat another bite of chicken."

And then came the long speeches.

"Do you wonder we were tired?" Louise Thaden later asked. "And perhaps a little irritable?"

BACK TO WICHITA

Pancho Barnes was more than a little irritable.

It was *killing* Pancho to watch the derby continue without her. Mechanics in Pecos had hoped to get her plane back in the air, but the wings were too badly damaged. The whole plane, they told her, would have to be shipped to the factory for major repairs.

Pancho was out of the race.

"I have flown that plane for two hundred hours," she told reporters. "I have flown it from coast to coast and from one border of the country to the other. Never before have I damaged it, and, of course, my first accident would have to come on an occasion of this kind."

The general rule was that if pilots hit something, it was their fault. In this case, Pancho angrily—and justifiably—blamed "that confounded automobile," driven by "some [bleep] hare-brained [bleep]."

Her face softened to what one paper described as a "wistful" expression as she added, "I'd just like to be in that race, even if to come in last."

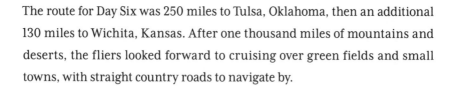

Fort Worth police officers patrolled the airfield all night. A police captain told papers, "We don't want those girls to leave Fort Worth thinking what they have at some of the other places at which they have stopped."

A crew from Walter Beech's factory also spent the night. There were four Travel Airs still in the race, including the planes flown by Louise Thaden and Blanche Noyes. From this point on, Beech wanted his own team with the planes every second they were on the ground.

Early the next morning, before the pilots arrived at the field, Margaret Perry's black-and-white Spartan came in for a landing. Still fighting a fever, she had gotten up before dawn in Abilene and flown to Fort Worth, desperate to rejoin the race.

Perry stumbled out of her plane, too dizzy to stand. She could barely see. Her temperature was 104. Rushed by ambulance to the nearest hospital, she was diagnosed with typhoid fever.

She *still* wouldn't quit the race. A doctor had to order her to stay in bed.

A reporter who dropped by to hear her story noted that Perry "choked back a sob" when she heard the drone of the derby planes passing over the hospital later that morning.

"For a pilot to be sick," she explained, "while her plane is working like a clock and champing its bits to go on with the race is the worst thing in the world."

The route for Day Six was 250 miles to Tulsa, Oklahoma, then an additional 130 miles to Wichita, Kansas. After one thousand miles of mountains and deserts, the fliers looked forward to cruising over green fields and small towns, with straight country roads to navigate by.

Louise Thaden, Gladys O'Donnell, Amelia Earhart, and Ruth Nichols were still bunched at the top of the standings, with four days of racing to go.

Ruth Elder started the day ninety minutes behind the leaders. She knew she wouldn't win, but she was closer to the front of the pack than the back—and a strong showing in the derby could only help her film career. Ruth's main worry, as she'd told reporters at the start of the race, was getting lost. And on her morning flight to Tulsa, just after she'd crossed the Red River into Oklahoma, it happened again.

"I was flying serenely along," she explained that evening, "when a gust of wind ripped my map to shreds, blowing most of it away, leaving me clutching a piece about as big as a postage stamp."

Ruth flew on for a few minutes with a sick feeling she was drifting off course. The only thing to do was land and ask for directions.

She set down in a pasture. A herd of cows looked up from the grass they'd been munching. As if curious about this visitor from the sky, the cows began jogging toward the plane.

It was a funny sight—until Ruth remembered an absurd little fact known only to pilots. Cows loved the taste of airplane dope, the glue used to secure fabric on airplane wings. They'd been known to chew fabric clean off the wings, leaving a bare wooden skeleton.

She needed to get out of there. But the cows were closing in. Waving a metal bar used to crank the motor, she chased the animals back, clearing a runway, then hopped into the cockpit, sped forward, climbed into the air, and headed north, in the general direction of Tulsa.

And she made it. She was the last one in, but she made it. The fans in Tulsa gave Elder a huge ovation as she zipped over the finish line. The other pilots, who'd started to worry, laughed along with Ruth as she explained the delay.

"It didn't make any difference anyway," she joked, "because I never could find anything on a map."

Midway through Day Six of the derby, the top of the heavy-plane division was as tight as it had ever been since the start:

RACER OVERALL TIME

Louise Thaden... 10:46:16
Ruth Nichols... 10:55:39
Gladys O'Donnell 10:57:55
Amelia Earhart 11:06:56

In the light-plane race, Phoebe Omlie held a comfortable lead over Edith Foltz, Chubbie Miller, and Thea Rasche. Rasche's clogged fuel line on Day Two had cost her hours, but she was determined to cross the finish line in Cleveland.

And, finally, Bobbi Trout was back in the air.

After three agonizing days of waiting in Yuma, Bobbi Trout left in her repaired plane, crossed Arizona and New Mexico, and headed into Texas.

"Sure, I'm gonna catch up," Bobbi said at an afternoon stop in El Paso.

Bobbi was out of the derby, in terms of official standings, but there was no way she was going to let the group get to Cleveland without her.

"At least," she said, "I will have the satisfaction of knowing I finished the race."

At the Tulsa airfield, the racers gathered on the roof of a hangar, waving to the cheering crowd as an announcer introduced the women one by one.

Race critic Erle Halliburton was there. He was not cheering.

"The Women's Air Derby is contributing nothing to aviation, and it should be canceled immediately," he told reporters, ramping up his campaign to stop the race. "Women are lacking in certain qualities that men possess, just as men are lacking in certain qualities that women possess. Handling essential to safe flying is one of the qualifications women have not mastered successfully."

Halliburton seemed particularly displeased with Ruth Elder, who had said in a recent interview that female pilots would soon fly for the military.

"If women," he said, "are going to pilot bombing planes in the next war, as Miss Ruth Elder predicted, I'd as soon be on one side as another."

Reporters asked the racers for a reaction to Halliburton's charges.

"Don't be foolish," Gladys O'Donnell fired back. "All the girls are competent pilots."

"I never heard of anything so ridiculous," Chubbie Miller added. "We'll show him we know our planes."

Amelia Earhart went on what was, for her, a furious rant.

"Who is this man Halliburton? Who is he to pass judgment on our ability?" Sure, she conceded, there had been accidents—but fewer than at any other cross-country race. "One thing I would like to call to his attention is that a greater percentage of the women flyers in *this* derby are still going. This is a better showing than has ever been the case in any men's race."

After lunch in Tulsa, the pilots trudged through dusty air to their planes. Louise Thaden had been first in, so she'd be first to leave for Wichita. Exactly where she needed to be.

It was only a few years since she'd spent summers in Wichita, an aimless college student selling coal and oil, sneaking away to watch airplanes take off and land. Now her family would be in Wichita to greet her. The whole Travel Air crew would be there. She needed her return to be triumphant.

Thaden sat in the cockpit, adjusting her goggles, checking her map, hands sweating, heart pumping. Her nerves always settled the moment she got in the air. Except this time they didn't.

One second she was laughing aloud, thinking, "It is magnificent to be alive! To ride down the lanes of the sky!"

The next she was shouting, "If I'm off course, I'll bash my head in!"

Battered by fierce headwinds, Thaden sped north into Kansas. She dropped the plane lower to get below the wind. That gave her a few more miles per hour, but the closer she got to the ground, the less she could see of the landscape around her. The less she could see, the harder it was to navigate. It was a trade-off she was willing to accept.

Hitting a rain shower at 150 miles per hour, the drops exploded on her glass windscreen and stung like bees on bare patches of skin. Her goggles fogged over, and she had to keep wiping them with her oil-stained scarf—it was either that or take off the goggles and squint. When the skies cleared a bit, she leaned over the side, wind ripping at her face as she peered north, straining to see the Wichita airfield she knew so well.

"There!" she shouted. "Over the tops of the trees, Louise, a flat space with buildings in the corner! It's *got* to be the airport!"

Thaden tore over the finish line. There were no other derby racers in sight.

"Atta baby," she said aloud, patting the side of her ship, "you smelled home, didn't you?"

As she circled the field, Louise felt the sudden urge to show off a bit, do a few stunts for the crowd. She resisted and came in for a smooth landing.

Even with the usual postflight ringing in her ears, she could hear car horns honking and the screaming of twenty-five thousand fans. At other stops, Ruth Elder and Amelia Earhart were the center of attention. This was Louise Thaden's moment.

Walter Beech—the man who'd given Louise her first job in aviation—led the crowd to her plane.

"Swell going, fella!" he hollered, chomping down on his pipe so enthusiastically the stem snapped in half.

"Hi, Pal! Pal!"

Louise recognized the voice. She jumped out of the plane and fought through the crowd to her father.

With two fast flights on Day Six, Louise Thaden upped her overall lead to thirty minutes. Gladys O'Donnell clung to second, with Ruth Nichols and Amelia Earhart still battling for third. Blanche Noyes sat in fifth place, and Ruth Elder, map troubles and all, held on in sixth.

Frank Copeland, one of the derby organizers, climbed onto a stage at the Wichita field and briefly interviewed each of the racers.

"The women are doing fine," Copeland then told the crowd, "and those who know what they are up against realize that they are demonstrating that women will take their part in the aviation development of the country."

Fans cheered and whistled and blasted car horns.

"We wish to thumb our collective noses at Halliburton!" Copeland roared. "There will be no stopping this race!"

At the Wichita airfield: The first three planes from right to left are Earhart's Vega, Thaden's Travel Air, and O'Donnell's Waco.

That same day, in San Diego, a much quieter crowd gathered for Marvel Crosson's funeral. The line stretched out the chapel door and down the block.

Marvel's parents were there, and her brother, Joe, and Emory, her fiancé. Her casket was covered with flowers. Friends and fellow fliers talked of Marvel's "radiant vitality" and "cheerful smile." Everyone agreed, it was hard to believe she was gone.

At a brief service, the Reverend Frank Linder praised Marvel's "courage and humbleness," saying, "It was not a desire for show, but a genuine love of adventure and for her life work which urged her on. Her deeds have made flying history. She has flown away to an unknown land."

"Not long ago," Linder continued, "she wrote a letter to the mother of a friend who had died in aviation."

The reverend had a copy of the letter. He read Marvel's words to the mourners:

"Don't worry. Every flyer would rather go out with her plane than suffer a more lingering death."

Race officials placed a large bouquet of flowers with Marvel's name on it in the lobby of the pilots' hotel in downtown Wichita.

Rumors of sabotage were still swirling. Reporters pressed the fliers to speculate.

Thea Rasche said she suspected "dirty work" early in the race. "Any one of thousands who might be interested in the race could have done the job," she charged, showing the now-famous "beware of sabotage" telegram.

Chubbie Miller wondered aloud about all the mishaps, but she did it with a smile. "And now," she said, laughing, "to cap it all, I have just about lost my voice from talking to so many people we have met along the way."

Thea Rasche and her stuffed monkey passenger.

Most of the pilots simply refused to talk about it.

Years later, many of the racers would say they *did* suspect the sabotage charges were founded. At the time, though, they feared that any talk of tampering with planes would only be fuel for those calling to cancel the race.

The racers cleaned up, changed, and joined four hundred guests on the hotel rooftop for the nightly banquet. One by one, the women rose to say a few words, mostly about how happy they were to be flying over farmland instead of mountains.

"I was glad I was able to come into Wichita in the lead," Louise Thaden said, "first, because it seems like home to me, having lived here, and second, because I am flying a Wichita ship."

"I am almost ashamed to talk to you," Ruth Elder began when it was her turn. "You see, I lost my map today." Ruth had the whole room howling as she told of her narrow escape from a crew of hungry cows. "You people can rest assured," she said in conclusion, "that from now on when I lose my map, I will have studied it enough so that I can fly without it."

Then came dinner—yes, chicken—speeches, music, and dancing until midnight. Most of the pilots slipped back to their rooms while the party was still going.

"Well, I feel now more like I'm getting somewhere!" Louise Thaden wrote in her race update that night. "There was nothing I wanted more than getting to Wichita first, unless it is to win this race to Cleveland."

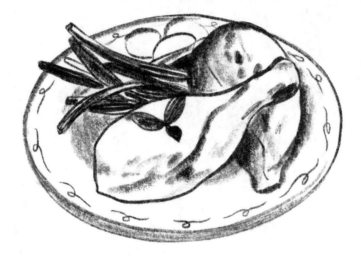

At the start of the race, when asked what the derby would come down to, she'd said, "A third the breaks, a third navigation, and a third the fastest ship."

She'd had the breaks so far—no mechanical issues or freak accidents. She'd navigated well through the hardest parts of the course, and she had one of the fastest planes.

It was a winning formula. The other racers were running out of time to catch her.

THE GRIND

Early the next morning, in the tea room of the pilots' Wichita hotel, Ruth Elder was enjoying a rare moment alone—until a *Wichita Eagle* reporter came searching for celebrity gossip.

Elder had long since divorced the man she'd been married to in Florida. She was young, single, and famous; every twist and turn of her personal life seemed to make the papers. According to the latest rumors, she was secretly engaged to a film producer named Walter Camp, Jr. The story was that Camp had proposed at Clover Field and that Elder had called the next day from San Bernardino with her answer.

Confronted in the tea room, Ruth confirmed the engagement. Reluctantly, she told the reporter, because she hadn't had a chance to tell her mother the news. She denied the part about accepting the proposal by phone.

"Mr. Camp is not a schoolboy," she said.

Newspapers *loved* stories like this about the derby racers. Even Gladys O'Donnell, the so-called "Flying Housewife," was the subject of scandalous rumor. When she got to the Wichita field that morning, Gladys read that she, too, was recently engaged, in her case to a New York City orchestra leader. This was an unpleasant surprise, both to her and her husband.

"Gladys O'Donnell," a reporter noted after checking with her, "said her plans did not include another wedding."

Her plans *did* include getting her plane ready for another day of racing. Her plans included catching Louise Thaden somewhere before Cleveland.

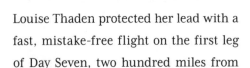

Louise Thaden protected her lead with a fast, mistake-free flight on the first leg of Day Seven, two hundred miles from Wichita to Kansas City.

"I'm pushing her," she told reporters at

FLIES WITH CUPID.

Derby Entrant To Marry If She Comes In First.

(By Pacific & Atlantic)
DAN CUPID'S boosting Miss Gladys O'Donnell (above) air derby racer. If she comes into Cleveland first, she announced yesterday at Wichita, she'll marry Abe Lipman, New York orchestra director. She is racing with Mrs. Louise Thaden for first place in the women's air race.

Gladys O'Donnell was quite surprised to read of her upcoming wedding. So was her husband.

the Kansas City airfield. "That cockpit was the hottest spot you ever knew."

It was another scorching summer day. Racers pulled off their leather helmets to give their sweaty hair a few minutes to dry. They gulped down water and rubbed lotion onto hands blistered from hours of gripping the planes' controls.

"Aye, your blithering deserts, do I like them?" Chubbie Miller asked reporters, pointing to her peeling nose. "Look you!"

The young Australian was becoming a fan favorite for her plucky attitude and quotable lines. One of the writers said she looked tired and asked if she needed to lie down.

"No, I shall not leave my plane until I see it serviced," Chubbie declared. "Bring on your oil and gas!"

Phoebe Omlie was sunburned, too, but refused to complain. "After the desert," she said of flying over the Midwest, "this is play."

Amelia Earhart didn't even get out of her plane. She had a quick snack, checked the weather report, looked over her map, and lined up for the second half of the day, 250 miles to East St. Louis, Illinois.

The sky turned gray and hazy as the planes sped across Missouri. The racers dropped low, watching the muddy Missouri River to stay on course. Using their watches, compasses, and airspeed indicators, the pilots knew about when and where to start looking for St. Louis. Spotting the tops of stone buildings rising from haze, they began searching the Illinois side of the Mississippi River for the East St. Louis airfield. Simply *finding* the clearings that qualified as early airports was one of the main challenges of the derby, especially when visibility was low. The crew in East St. Louis placed lighted lanterns along the foggy strip, which saved many of the racers from flying past.

Louise Thaden circled the field, studying it, hating it. It was short and cramped, with a road along one side and electrical wires strung between poles at the far end.

"I came in as slowly as I could," she recalled, "quite low over the road."

She was about to skim over the road when a wagon rolled up—with a man standing in the back, looking up. Swerving over the man's head, she found herself instantly above the little field, too far down the field to land safely—but flying too slowly to climb and clear the wires ahead.

"I'm going to overshoot!"

Her only hope was to pancake in. She slammed down to the grass with her feet on the brakes. The plane skidded to a stop below the electrical wires.

Thaden sat for a long moment in her cockpit, letting the panic drain, just trying to breathe.

179

Battling for the lead on Day Seven: Louise Thaden, Gladys O'Donnell, and Ruth Nichols.

Bobbi Trout landed in Wichita at seven thirty that evening.

"Can I catch them in St. Louis in the morning?" she asked the airport crew.

There was a good chance she could. She'd flown all the way from Pecos in one day, with stops in Midland, Abilene, Fort Worth, and Tulsa. Bobbi would have loved to have caught up with the racers that evening, but she refused to cut corners by skipping any stop along the route.

Besides, she wasn't sorry to miss yet another banquet.

"She said she did not care particularly for banquets at any time," reported the *Wichita Eagle*, "and that in most of the towns the girls were given too much banqueting for their own good."

★

In New York City, a reporter cornered Walter Camp to ask about his engagement to Ruth Elder. "Will Miss Elder do any more flying?"

"No, except perhaps a few flights for pleasure," Camp declared. "There won't be any more of this sort of thing."

"Will she continue to work in the movies?"

"Positively not," he said. "Boots is perfectly satisfied to settle down and be Mrs. Camp."

He probably should have checked with Boots.

Day Seven was in the books. Louise Thaden held tight to the lead, with Gladys O'Donnell, Ruth Nichols, and Amelia Earhart well within striking distance.

RACER OVERALL TIME

Louise Thaden.. 16:27:57
Gladys O'Donnell 17:14:33
Ruth Nichols... 17:50:37
Amelia Earhart 17:57:21

"Well, here we are," Louise wrote that night in East St. Louis, "just two days from the finish."

They'd all made it through another day. Another banquet. Another plate of chicken.

"The trip has been a terrible grind, and I am so tired I can hardly hold my head up tonight." She'd been working so hard and sweating so much she was down ten pounds since leaving Santa Monica. And for every hour in the air, she explained, the racers were spending several more studying maps and working on their planes. "A very small portion of the flying is done in

the air. If you don't check things yourself, there is going to be something to go wrong."

Tomorrow was another long day—over four hundred miles across Illinois and Indiana, then northeast into Ohio, with a final stop at Columbus. From there, it was just 120 miles to the finish line.

"Oh, yes," she added at the end of the article, as if just now remembering she hadn't seen her husband, Herb, in a week. "I am going to meet my sweetheart in Columbus tomorrow night, and I certainly will be glad to see him."

Louise Thaden woke up nervous, anxious to get going. The hotel restaurant wasn't open, so she left for the airfield without breakfast. When she got there, the field was covered in morning fog. Gray mist swirled around the mechanics at work, blurring them to ghostly forms.

But the *really* scary thing was that someone had messed with her plane.

Making his early-morning checks, Travel Air mechanic Johnnie Burke had discovered damage to the motor's two magnetos, vital parts that generate electricity for the spark plugs. The main threat to Louise Thaden's lead was a forced landing because of mechanical failure. Here was a problem that could stop her engine cold.

She suggested that it might be a normal malfunction. Burke did not agree. He showed her the damage, pointing out breaker points that seemed, to his expert eye, to have been purposely filed down.

Years later, Thaden would guess that her lead in the derby had something to do with her plane's being targeted. But at the time, talk of sabotage had died down. She wanted to keep it that way. She wanted nothing to stop the successful completion of the race.

Burke quietly fixed the plane. He promised her that that night, in Columbus, he'd sleep in the cockpit.

The fog burned off, and the racers zipped over cars, trucks, and trains on their way across Illinois.

A crowd of ten thousand cheered as the planes landed at Dresser Field in Terre Haute, Indiana, the day's first stop. Friendly fans had set up a large tent for the racers, with chairs and a few cots and a table piled with cheese and chicken sandwiches.

They couldn't understand why the pilots took only the cheese.

With a few minutes before the next flight, the racers collapsed onto the cots and chairs.

"Hey," Phoebe Omlie grumbled, "get your foot out of my face!"

Amelia Earhart moved her foot.

As soon as they got comfortable, the starter announced it was time to go. Ruth Elder quickly touched up her makeup. The other women were grateful to her for drawing the attention of photographers away from their own grimy faces.

"Good luck, everybody!" they called to each other as they walked to their planes.

George Putnam, Amelia Earhart's publisher and promoter, met the racers at the day's second stop, Cincinnati, Ohio.

Putnam monitored every detail of Earhart's career, even sending her harsh critiques of photos that appeared in newspapers—telling her, for instance, to smile with her mouth closed to hide the gap between her two front teeth. He'd even started spinning Earhart's reputation as a pilot. About a year before the derby, when she made a rough landing at a Pittsburgh field, he immediately put out a statement to the press:

"Miss Earhart had made a perfect landing when the plane struck an unmarked ditch and went into it. Miss Earhart feels it is unfortunate that the accident should have happened, particularly as it occurred through no fault of hers."

Putnam had been very worried about how Amelia would do in the derby. At Cincinnati, she was in fourth place—very respectable, considering the competition. But it was not the result he wanted. He seemed unhappy.

After a quick lunch, Putnam and a friend took off for Columbus in a small plane. The plane's engine died, and the ship tore through branches on its way to a hard landing in a cornfield. Putnam and his friend stumbled out of the wreck.

They were rubbing their bruises when the derby planes roared overhead. Spotting Earhart's red Vega, Putnam started jumping up and down, waving for help.

She sped right past.

When he complained to her that night, she said she hadn't seen him.

"If you'd sighted the wrecked plane, would you have come back?" he asked.

No, she said. "Not if I'd seen you were all in one piece."

Edith Foltz, holding second place in the light-plane division, never crossed the finish line in Cincinnati. The little airfield was sunk in a valley beside a bend in the Ohio River that didn't match anything on her road map; she simply couldn't find it. Foltz circled and searched, then continued on to Columbus. She was disqualified for missing the stop.

Bobbi Trout made it to Cincinnati an hour after the racers left. She refueled, got back in the air, and was finally about to catch up—when her engine died again. As she glided down to a field, her right wing scraped a fence post, ripping a hole in the fabric.

Time to give up? Hardly. Somehow patching her wing with a flattened tin can and a piece of wire, Bobbi took off and continued the chase.

In Wichita, Louise Thaden's father awaited news of each leg of the derby with growing anticipation.

"I have all the confidence in the world that Louise will win the derby," Roy McPhetridge told the *Wichita Eagle*, "but I never like to count my chickens before they're hatched. There are some mighty good fliers in the derby, and anything is liable to happen."

In Cleveland, the roads leading to the airport were jammed with traffic. Over one hundred thousand people showed up for the opening of the 1929 National Air Races and Aeronautical Exposition.

The weeklong event would include stunt flights, famous pilots, flying contests, parachute-jumping contests, displays of the latest aviation technology, and the finish of men's long-distance races coming in from Miami, Oakland, and Portland, Oregon. It was the largest aviation event ever held. And it was all very festive, noted the *New York Times*, but "chief interest here centers in the Women's Derby."

The racers were due in Cleveland the next day.

The last leg of Day Eight, Cincinnati to Columbus, was easy to navigate, with large roads and towns along the way. An enthusiastic farmer even cut an arrow-shaped clearing in his corn field, pointing the way to Columbus.

Louise Thaden felt her entire body tingle as she rocketed over the finish line. She *knew* no one had gained on her. She had resisted the urge to show off in Wichita, but now, with her husband down there watching, she couldn't hold back. Louise flipped over and flew upside-down. She flew loop-the-loops. She climbed and dove toward the field in a screaming spin, pulling out just above the crowd.

"See that Herb!" she whooped in the air. "Aren't you proud of your wife's flying?"

A crowd of twenty thousand shoved through a line of police as Thaden coasted in for a perfect landing.

"Look this way, Mrs. Thaden!" photographers cried.

"Hey, Louise, look this way!"

People were everywhere, shouts and smiling faces. But she couldn't see Herb. He wasn't there. She was crushed.

Other racers landed. Fans and photographers left Louise to mob the other planes.

Five long minutes later, Herb strolled up, casually calling, "Hello, dear!"

"Well, Herb. Did you just arrive?"

"Oh, no," he said. "I've been here an hour."

"Did you see the show I put on for you?"

He had not. "I've been back in the hangar," he said, "shooting the breeze with some mechanics."

For a passing moment, according to Thaden family lore, she wanted to kill him.

The derby manager in Columbus had been warned to avoid chicken.

"You can have anything you want to eat, even if it's hot dogs," he announced to the happy racers. "That is, just so you don't order champagne and lobsters."

Unfortunately for the pilots, the banquet had been planned far in advance. The elegantly printed menu listed the main dish as . . .

"Breast of Chicken on Toast"

Luckily there were other dishes: Kentucky ham, Parisienne potatoes, mushrooms in supreme sauce, tomatoes with French dressing, and a dessert called "Airplane Ice Cream."

After attending the banquet with Herb, Louise Thaden sat down to finish one last race update. "Somehow this final night together is tinged with sadness," she wrote. "For months before the derby started, we were only names to each other. Now we've become something more, for trouble and tragedy has dogged us from the very start of the race."

She spoke again of Marvel Crosson's death, and about how Marvel continued to inspire the racers, to bond them tighter. "We feel that Marvel's

sacrifice was not in vain if it proved nothing other than women had the nerve to continue even when tragedy was thrust in their faces."

"Well, tomorrow tells the tale," she concluded. "I'm going to give the old ship everything it has to get to Cleveland first."

Out at the airfield, Johnnie Burke spent a sleepless night in the cockpit of Louise Thaden's plane.

FINISH LINE

The last leg of the derby was scheduled for a 1:00 pm start. For once, Ruth Nichols could have slept in, caught up on sleep. Instead, she drove to the airport at dawn.

After a cautious start, Nichols had moved steadily up the standings. With one final push in mind, she'd asked the mechanics at Columbus to tune up her Rearwin overnight, giving it every ounce of possible speed. The work was done, and now she climbed into the plane for a quick test flight.

She was thrilled. "Never had the motor run better," she'd later say, "smooth as butter."

Nichols was clinging to third place, two minutes ahead of Amelia Earhart. And more than bragging rights were at stake—the $875 prize for third place was more than most women could earn in six months. The way her motor was humming, Nichols was going to hold off Amelia, maybe even catch Gladys O'Donnell or Louise Thaden if they opened the door.

She circled the field one last time, studying it in preparation for landing.

The paved runway was still under construction, with tractors and steamrollers parked along the unfinished edges. Nichols turned her plane into the wind, the standard procedure for landing—wind flowing over the wings provides lift, which allows a plane to fly safely at a slower speed as it comes in for the landing.

But the wind shifted just as the wheels of Nichols's plane touched the pavement. A gust whipped across the runway, tossing the plane sideways. The wings clipped a steamroller, and the Rearwin spun two full cartwheels, shedding parts, before slamming to a stop on its back.

A man on the construction crew ran up, shouting, "Are you hurt, Sis?"

Nichols dangled upside-down in her open cabin, held in place by her seat belt. Incredibly, she was only bruised. "But get me out, quick, before the gasoline explodes!"

He yanked her out of the wreck, and they backed away. The plane never did explode, but it was ruined. Nichols stood, hands on hips and heartbroken, staring at the scattered remains of her beautiful ship.

Ruth Nichols's race ended in an instant, just 120 miles short of the finish line.

She was one of the best pilots in the derby—and just like that, it was over. Ruth Nichols was out of the race.

"How's she running, Johnnie?" Louise Thaden asked when she got to her plane that morning.

The mechanic grinned with pride.

Still, with 120 miles to go, anything could happen.

"Now don't get excited—take it easy," Herb Thaden said. "You aren't worried, are you? How do you feel? Are your maps okay? Don't let Ruth's crack-up bother you."

"Herb," Louise said, "if you'll leave me alone, I'll be all right."

"Okay, dear. Has your ship been gassed? Do you know what your compass course is? You'll be careful, won't you? Not get over-anxious and do something foolish?"

The main thing making her anxious was him.

He checked his watch for the hundredth time. "You'll get to Cleveland all right, just don't get all upset and excited. Don't you think it's time to warm up the engine?"

Louise climbed into her cockpit. She strapped herself in and started her motor.

Herb, standing alone by the wing, looked so nervous she felt sorry for him.

On Day Nine, pilots would take off in the order of the overall standings. The idea was to give the leading planes the honor of getting to Cleveland first.

A race official strode up. "Mrs. Thaden, you are first off. Be careful, your ship is near the edge of the runway. We will give you the customary ten-count. Good luck."

"Thanks," Louise said, reaching out to shake hands.

The starter waved his flags—*one, two, three* . . .

Louise tried to swallow. Her throat felt swollen and blocked. She'd flown so well for eight straight days. What if her engine quit now? What if she got lost? It was the wrong time for these thoughts, but she couldn't shake them.

Eight, nine, ten!

The starter's white flag fell. Thaden's plane shot forward, lifted off the ground, climbed, and turned northeast.

For a fast plane like hers, Cleveland was less than an hour away.

At Cleveland Airport, boys worked through the crowd, selling amber-tinted glasses to race fans who wanted to gaze into the sky to watch for incoming racers.

Pancho Barnes was there—as a fan. She'd borrowed a plane to get to Cleveland in time to watch the end of the derby. "I've been flying airplanes too long to be satisfied with train travel," she told a reporter.

Elinor Smith, the teenage flier, was there. Unable to get a plane for the derby, Smith had accepted a job flying stunts for the crowds in Cleveland.

Charles Lindbergh, the famous Atlantic flier, was there—but not necessarily to cheer on the Women's Air Derby. A reporter asked him, "Is aviation a woman's game?"

He frowned. "I haven't anything to say about that. I'm sorry."

"Halfway there," Louise Thaden said aloud, "and making good time."

She was flying with her map on her lap, looking back and forth between the map and her compass, between cockpit gauges and the landscape below, raging at every little breeze that moved her a foot off course.

"Take it easy," she told herself. "You can cruise over and win from here."

But she couldn't shake the pins and needles.

The last few weeks had been such a roller-coaster ride. Those sleepless nights waiting for her plane to be built and then nearly dying on her way to the starting line. The long days of racing and late nights of writing articles and studying maps. The endless banquets, the tasteless chicken. The fears of sabotage. The vicious race critics. Those terrifying crashes of Pancho Barnes and Ruth Nichols, and the shock of Marvel's death.

"Keep working!" she commanded her motor. "Keep working until we get to Cleveland, and then I don't care what you do."

Suddenly deciding to play it safe, Thaden eased back on the throttle, slowing the plane.

It didn't feel right. She opened the throttle.

Every few seconds, she looked for the airport, knowing she couldn't possibly be close enough yet to see it. But she *must* be on course—people were watching and waving from the roofs of houses and barns.

The vast blue surface of Lake Erie came into view.

Then the city of Cleveland.

And there it was—the airport! A tall control tower and huge hangars. Crowds in grandstands leaping to their feet. A white line of chalk across a wide grass field.

Louise Thaden put her nose down and roared over the finish line at 170 miles per hour.

Reporters and photographers dashed onto the field, swarming Thaden's plane before the propeller stopped spinning.

"Mrs. Thaden, how does it feel, having won the first Women's Air Derby?"

"Hi, Louise, congratulations!"

"Can we get an endorsement from you of Firebrand Tires?"

"Stay in the ship!"

"Please get out of the cockpit!"

Louise pulled off her leather helmet and shook out her sweat-soaked hair. Her ears were ringing. She looked up at grandstands full of cheering fans. Cliff Henderson, director of the National Air Races, ran up with a massive, horseshoe-shaped flower arrangement.

"Put it over your head!" photographers shouted.

Thaden tried, but the thing was almost as big as she was. And the rose stems were thick with thorns. She sat in her cockpit, smiling for the cameras as sharp barbs pierced the back of her neck.

The race announcer stuck a microphone in her face. Movie cameras were rolling. Everyone was staring at her. She felt as if she'd just woken from a dream.

The announcer poked her. "For heaven's sake, say something!"

"Hello, folks," Louise said, her voice echoing over the loudspeakers. "The sunburn derby is over, and I happened to come in first. I happen to come in first not because I'm a better pilot than any of the rest of the girls, but because I have a fast airplane and I had good breaks."

Then Thaden climbed out of the cockpit and set the bouquet of roses on the front of her plane.

Gladys O'Donnell flashed over the line in second place. Fans swarmed her plane as she taxied to a stop. Reporters wanted to know if she was "thrilled" by her second-place finish.

"Thrilled?" O'Donnell asked. "Well, I'm awfully glad to be here, but I could be a lot more thrilled if I was in first place."

The crowd shouted again as Amelia Earhart's red Vega sped over the finish line in third.

Earhart then circled the field and descended toward the runway, coming in fast. The plane bounced down the grass, using most of the long landing

Louise Thaden salutes the crowd in Cleveland.

strip before skidding to a stop. As Amelia flipped open the top of her cockpit and waved to the grandstands, Elinor Smith, watching from the stands, overheard a few nasty cracks about the rough landing.

"But at that moment, I was filled with admiration for her," Smith would later say. Amelia Earhart had taken a huge risk, both to her reputation and her life, by racing in the Vega. Third place was a real accomplishment.

The crowd greeted Cleveland-born Blanche Noyes with thunderous ovation for her fourth-place finish. An ecstatic Dewey Noyes sprinted to his wife's plane. Eager to get the celebration started, he stuck a cigar in his mouth and lit a match.

"Don't light that here!" Blanche ordered, still spooked by the cigarette in her luggage compartment.

Dewey blew out the match.

"A wonderful, wonderful experience," was how Blanche described the derby to reporters. "For myself, I don't mind that I didn't win. Mrs. Thaden is a peach." She was amazed, she said, at all the attention the women had gotten along the way. "I think I've autographed everything but flypaper."

"Now the thing I'm interested in is sleep," Blanche added. "I hardly got any during the race."

Phoebe Omlie landed fifth, crushing her competition in the light-plane division. Even with metal braces on both legs, Omlie flew such a flawless race she finished ahead of six of the faster planes.

Thea Rasche, battling clogged gas lines and sabotage fears all the way across the country, cruised into Cleveland to grab second place in the light-plane division.

Chubbie Miller zipped in to take third. "I saw this nice field with a lot of grass and I just sat down in it," Chubbie said with a grin, describing a forced landing that had delayed her arrival. "I missed some horses, cows, and pigs, and skipped a couple of ditches, but neither the plane nor I was damaged."

By about three, all the racers were in—except for Ruth Elder. Pilots and fans were starting to get worried when they saw another plane diving toward the field. But it wasn't Elder.

It was Bobbi Trout!

Finally catching up after four days of pursuit, Bobbi's Golden Eagle sped over the finish line.

Then another roar from the crowd—Ruth Elder was coming in. Fans gave her a standing ovation, then charged her plane, surrounding her, waving pieces of paper for her to sign.

Asked about the delay, Ruth laughed. Basically, she explained, she'd flown by mistake to Akron. In need of directions, she'd landed in a field—which turned out to be on the grounds of a prison.

"Well," she joked, "people always said I'd wind up in prison."

Even with the slow last day, Ruth Elder finished a strong fifth out of ten in the fast-plane division.

FINAL STANDINGS: HEAVY PLANES
RACER OVERALL TIME

Louise Thaden.. 20:19:20
Gladys O'Donnell 21:21:42
Amelia Earhart 22:12:42
Blanche Noyes 24:33:58
Ruth Elder... 28:17:23
Neva Paris... 29:29:29
Mary von Mach.. 30:57:23
May Haizlip 33:12:02
Opal Kunz... 33:12:04
Vera Dawn Walker................................. 35:14:32*

*Walker's time into Columbus. Her final time doesn't seem to have been recorded, but it would have been about an hour more than this.

LIGHT PLANES
RACER OVERALL TIME

Phoebe Omlie.. 25:12:47
Thea Rasche... 31:12:36
Chubbie Miller 53:02:44

Edith Foltz finished but was disqualified for missing Cincinnati. Bobbi Trout finished, untimed.

Fifteen of the twenty pilots who'd started the Women's Air Derby made it to the finish line. This was the highest percentage of finishers in any cross-country air race to date.

"I'm frank to admit," said race official Frank Copeland, "that not many men could have gotten out of some of the mechanical and navigational difficulties we have encountered."

Cliff Henderson, who'd resisted calls to cancel the derby, agreed. "If ever there was a question as to women's ability to fly, and to take a significant part in this great industry, it is now definitely and finally settled."

After a half hour in front of cameras and microphones, Louise Thaden slipped into the airport terminal and sent a telegram to her family:

LANDED OK CLEVELAND FIRST LOVE LOUISE

"I was rather confident she would win," her father declared. "But, of course, the suspense makes one rather nervous."

Thaden, Gladys O'Donnell, and Blanche Noyes found an empty office and collapsed on couches, savoring their success for a quiet moment. It wasn't long before reporters barged in.

"How was the race?" one asked.

"You'll have to talk louder," Thaden said. "I can hardly hear out of these ears."

"How much do you want for your story of the trip? I'll write it."

"Not interested."

Louise didn't need anyone to write her story. She'd been writing articles all along and was already contracted for more.

"Don't you feel pretty happy?"

Sure, Louise said, but she'd had the breaks and a fast plane. "It's no credit on my part—"

"Oh, yes it is," Gladys cut in.

"It certainly is," Blanche added.

Then it was time for one last banquet.

Gladys O'Donnell had nothing to wear. Back at Clover Field, she'd promised to take nothing fancier than her pilot coveralls, and she'd meant it.

Stained and splattered after nine days in the air, it was the only outfit she had. A Cleveland department store owner invited Gladys to come and pick anything from his dress department, anything at all, free of charge.

She went to the store. Nothing looked right. She wore her flying clothes to the ball.

Bobbi Trout had lost her luggage somewhere along the route. She hadn't changed in a week. Elinor Smith, who'd twice broken Bobbi's endurance records, loaned Bobbi a clean white shirt. Bobbi showed up at the banquet in the shirt—and dirty pants and boots. The two rivals began toying with the idea of working together to set an endurance record as a team.

Pancho Barnes was back to her usual self, cracking jokes, looking ahead to her next adventure. For weeks she'd been hearing rumors that Walter Beech was about to unveil a new plane, even faster than the one Pancho had wrecked in Texas, a model so secret it was spoken of as the "Mystery Ship." Pancho decided she'd buy one and see what it could do.

There seemed to be some tension between Amelia Earhart and George Putnam.

"Much later," Elinor Smith recalled, "I heard through the New York grapevine that Putnam was acidly critical of her performance in the race—but only to her. To everyone else, he blamed her poor showing on the airplane."

To the pilots, it was ridiculous to call Amelia's third-place finish a poor showing, especially given her lack of experience in powerful planes. Besides, Amelia Earhart was all about the bigger picture, the larger goal of proving there was no limit on what women could do. In that sense, she'd helped make the derby a smashing success.

And the experience would prove useful. Amelia Earhart was now a better and more confident pilot. Next, she decided, she'd fly across the Atlantic Ocean again. This time, solo.

Ruth Nichols, who made it to Cleveland in time for the banquet, had the exact same plan. Amelia had beaten her across the Atlantic once; she was not going to let it happen again.

Louise Thaden was finally beginning to relax. Herb, too. He'd seemed more nervous than anyone that morning, but there was no sign of that now.

"I was sure she'd win," Herb crowed. "She is an excellent pilot."

Louise Thaden, in her quietly determined way, had done everything she'd set out to do.

"I think we have proved," she said, "that we can fly as long, as hard, and consistently, and as well as the men." Standing to accept the trophy for winning the first Women's Air Derby, Louise repeated her promise to have the silver cup inscribed with the name Marvel Crosson and sent to Marvel's parents.

"Wherever she now is, we know that *she* knows the things we would like to say and can find no words to express," Louise would write a few days later. "Pioneers can only look forward, never back—so each of us carried on and flew perhaps a little better race than we had thought possible."

RACING THE ATLANTIC, THE SEQUEL

"It is almost impossible to realize that I'm in Cleveland and that I got here first," Louise Thaden wrote in her final derby article for the *Wichita Eagle*. "My heart's desire has been realized. I am very happy."

But the joy was mixed with sadness, reluctance to accept the experience was over. "These new friendships will make it hard to bear the thought of a parting of the ways," she wrote. "They are real friendships formed as members of a band set apart practically from the whole world."

The band should stick together, the pilots decided. Before leaving Cleveland, the racers agreed to form an organization of female pilots. Formally founded later that year, the group called itself the Ninety-Nines—for its ninety-nine original members. The Ninety-Nines are still going strong today, with thousands of members in forty-four countries.

That fall, Louise Thaden and Amelia Earhart spent a weekend with Ruth Nichols at Ruth's home in Rye, New York. After dinner one night, the conversation turned from derby memories to childhood stories, and

Louise and Amelia traded tales of tomboy adventures. Louise proudly announced she'd been able to whip any boy in wrestling. Amelia said she could do the same.

They looked at each other. They were thinking the same thing.

Ruth said she'd be the referee.

Clearing enough room for two tall women to battle, the wrestling match began. It did not go the way Louise expected. "We huffed and we puffed, and A.E. finally blew my house in," Thaden later confessed. "Her strength was absolutely amazing."

These were ambitious and competitive women. Women who could not sit still. Not even after a pleasant meal. As Louise Thaden said soon after the derby, "I think we would be willing to go again next month."

★

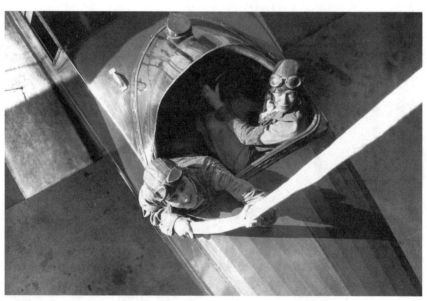

On the ground, Bobbi Trout grabs the gas hose, and Elinor Smith takes the controls as the team practices for their endurance flight.

Bobbi Trout and Elinor Smith felt the same.

Elinor spent the fall of 1929 with Bobbi's family in Los Angeles, preparing for the first women's refueling endurance flight. On their first try, they'd been flying for twelve hours when disaster struck. Elinor had the controls, and Bobbi was handling the incredibly dangerous job of standing in the open cockpit while a plane flying above tossed down a gas hose. Bobbi caught it and was pumping gas into their tanks when the supply plane hit turbulence and lurched downward. Elinor dove to avoid a midair collision, and the gas nozzle swung loose, spraying gas into Bobbi's open mouth. They landed, and Bobbi was rushed to the hospital, barely able to breathe. Friends urged her to quit.

She was back at the field the next morning.

Taking four-hour shifts at the controls, sleeping on top of gas tanks in the nose of the plane, Elinor Smith and Bobbi Trout stayed in the air for forty-two hours and five minutes—and only came back to earth because the refueling plane broke down.

Now doing it for real—Bobbi Trout and Elinor Smith refuel during their record endurance flight.

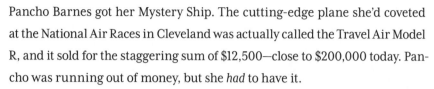

Pancho Barnes got her Mystery Ship. The cutting-edge plane she'd coveted at the National Air Races in Cleveland was actually called the Travel Air Model R, and it sold for the staggering sum of $12,500—close to $200,000 today. Pancho was running out of money, but she *had* to have it.

Her timing was excellent. When the plane was delivered in the summer of 1930, Amelia Earhart had just set a new women's speed record of 184 miles per hour. Pancho immediately shattered the mark in her Mystery Ship, topping out at 196 miles per hour.

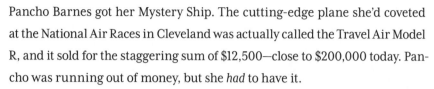

The big prize was still sitting out there. Which woman would go down in history as the first to fly solo across the Atlantic Ocean?

By the spring of 1931, Amelia Earhart and Elinor Smith both had Atlantic plans in the works. Ruth Nichols beat them in the race to find sponsors and adapt a plane for the long, nonstop flight.

"Yes, Ruth is bound and determined to do this desperate thing," her mother told friends in New York. "I just don't know what we are going to do about that girl. I've tried to reason with her, but it is no use. These modern girls think nothing is impossible."

On June 22, 1931, under clear blue skies, Ruth took off for what would be her starting point—Newfoundland, Canada, which is hundreds of miles closer to Europe than the northeastern United States. Four hours after leaving New York, she approached her first planned stop, New Brunswick, Canada. She'd been told the airfield there was big enough for her Lockheed Vega. When it came into view, she thought she must be off course. The tiny field looked like the bottom of a bowl, hemmed in by forested slopes. She double-checked her map.

Her heart sank. The sun was dropping behind the hills. There was nowhere else to land.

Nichols turned her plane into the wind. Skimming over the trees and into the bowl, her wheels were about to touch earth—but the rocky ridge on the far edge of the field was coming up fast, too fast, and there would be no way to stop in time. Nichols opened the throttle and tried to climb. She was just about clear when she heard the sickening smack of her tail hitting a tree branch.

The plane went down in the trees. Nichols undid her safety belt, opened the cockpit hatch, and pulled herself onto the wing, pain piercing her back like stabs from a flaming blade.

A news photographer stood in the bushes beside the wreck, snapping pictures.

Other, more helpful, men came running from the airfield. They carried her to the airport and put her in a taxi to the nearest hospital. As she was being wheeled down the hospital hallway, Nichols dictated a telegram to her mother.

"All I did was wrench my back and wreck the ship. Everything under control. Awfully sorry about the crack-up. Will do it next time. Love, Ruth."

After being taken for X-rays, she was lying in bed, planning how to rebuild her plane, when a doctor strode in.

"My dear young lady," he said, "I hope you know how lucky you are to be alive."

"Just how bad is it, doctor?"

"We'll patch you up good as new," he assured her. "You'll be walking, playing golf, even maybe flying again—in about a year."

"A *year!*" she howled. "I've got to fly the Atlantic!"

That would have to wait, he explained. She had five broken bones in her back.

Ruth Nichols refused to give up. That fall, against medical advice, she made plans to fly across the ocean with her body in a metal brace. Only twenty-five straight days of rain over the eastern Atlantic forced her to postpone.

Nichols geared up to try again in the spring of 1932. In May, waiting for a few last tune-ups to her plane, she had lunch with Amelia Earhart. It was awkward; each knew the other was about to try the Atlantic flight.

"You know, Ruth," Amelia said, "I always feel that you have to take some chances on long-distance flights, so I don't bother to go into all the possible accidents that might happen. I just don't think about crack-ups."

Two days later, May 21, Ruth Nichols's plane was ready. She opened the paper that morning to see the headline:

AMELIA EARHART OFF ON OCEAN FLIGHT

Earhart's red Lockheed Vega was twelve thousand feet over the Atlantic. Her plan was to fly through the night and reach Europe in daylight.

It was smooth sailing until 11:00 PM, when storm clouds slid over the moon and stars. Violent turbulence tossed her plane around, and the only thing visible through the windshield was the occasional streak of lightning. She battled the storm for hours, not seeing but *feeling* ice forming on her wings, feeling the sluggishness of the ship.

Diving for warmer air, with zero visibility ahead, she watched the needle of her altimeter gauge spinning uselessly, clearly broken. She got lucky, bursting through the clouds before hitting the sea, so low she could see bubbles of white foam on the tops of the black waves. For the rest of the night, she flew in the low-ceilinged tunnel between cloud cover and water, sipping tomato juice through a straw, no appetite for food. Ten hours into the flight, the skies cleared. As the sun rose, she reached for her sunglasses.

Earhart's plan had been to reach Paris, but fuel was running low. A gas line from a reserve tank in the cabin was leaking, dripping onto the left shoulder of her leather jacket. An exhaust pipe was cracked, vibrating more and more as it came loose. She had to put the plane down. Judging wind direction by the spray on the tops of the waves, she reset her heading, aiming now for Ireland.

After two more tense hours, Earhart spotted land rising from the sea, a hilly coast—covered with a thunderstorm she knew she'd better not try to fly through. Turning north along the coast, she followed railroad tracks to a city she later learned was Londonderry, Ireland. With no airport in sight, she found an empty field. Empty except for cows. Amelia buzzed low over the field, forcing the cows to clear a path. She landed on the grass.

She checked her watch. She'd been in the air just over fifteen hours.

A farmhand walked up, staring at the strange sight of an airplane in the meadow.

Amelia Earhart opened the cockpit and jumped to the ground.

"Where am I?" she asked.

"In Gallagher's pasture," the man said. "Have you come far?"

She smiled. "I've come from America."

Amelia Earhart's solo flight from Canada to this field in Ireland catapulted her to a whole new level of fame.

EPILOGUE

THE RACE GOES ON

Ruth Nichols sat by her radio all night and into the morning. When news of Earhart's arrival in Ireland was finally broadcast, she was glad to hear her friend was safe. But the stronger emotion was crushing disappointment at missing another chance to make history.

"I felt pretty low," she'd later say.

Rallying her spirits, she sent a telegram to Ireland: "You beat me to it for the second time, but it was a splendid job. My greatest admiration for your planning and skill in carrying out the hop. Love, Ruth."

For Amelia Earhart, the response to her second Atlantic flight was even bigger than her first—parades, honors, speeches, and fame *far* beyond that of her friends and rivals.

For Ruth Nichols, the only thing to do was to get back in the air.

Nichols went on to break a long list of flying records in the 1930s. In 1940, she founded Relief Wings, an organization of volunteer pilots dedicated to emergency air rescue and disaster relief on the home front during World War II. In 1958, she flew a US Air Force Delta Dagger at one thousand miles per hour and to an altitude of fifty-one thousand feet, both new marks for women.

In a lifetime of flying, Nichols suffered *six* serious crashes. But for the woman who had grown up terrified of heights, there was never any question of coming down.

"Family and friends have urged me to keep my feet on the ground ever since the first time I came home in an ambulance," Ruth Nichols wrote in her memoir, *Wings for Life*. "The only people who haven't tried to change me are flyers."

There never was another race like the first Women's Air Derby.

In late October 1929, just two months after the end of the derby, the Roaring Twenties came crashing to an end. The stock market collapsed, companies folded, banks failed, families lost their life savings, and unemployment soared. In the catastrophe that became known as the Dust Bowl, drought struck the Great Plains, and wind blew topsoil into the sky, driving farm families from their land in desperate search of jobs that didn't exist. The Great Depression brought ten years of economic misery, changing life for everyone—including female pilots, who found it much tougher to get sponsors for races or land jobs demonstrating planes no one had the money to buy.

Gladys O'Donnell entered the 1930 women's cross-country derby, but it was a smaller race than the year before, with none of the other fliers from the 1929 derby and a fraction of the media coverage. O'Donnell dominated the race, winning by five hours. She went on to become a flight instructor and movie stunt flier.

Typical of the times, newspapers continued to call her "The Flying Housewife."

Blanche Noyes went home to Ohio and was hired as a pilot for Standard

Oil. In 1930, she took the company's founder and world's richest man, John D. Rockefeller, who was ninety and terrified of planes, on his first and only airplane trip.

Two of the derby racers, Claire Fahy and Neva Paris, died in plane crashes in 1930.

Undaunted, the others continued pushing limits, breaking through barriers. Margaret Perry operated an airport in California. Vera Dawn Walker and May Haizlip took dangerous jobs as test pilots, flying new aircraft for airplane makers. Opal Kunz's proudest memory was teaching more than four hundred young men to fly for the US Army Air Corps during World War II.

During the 1932 presidential election campaign, Franklin D. Roosevelt, governor of New York, promised to attack the Depression with programs he called the New Deal. Eleanor Roosevelt, his wife—and one of his key political strategists—decided to find a pilot to help Franklin get elected. She turned to Phoebe Omlie.

In a groundbreaking piece of presidential campaigning, Omlie flew over five thousand miles, stopping in twelve states, with the slogan "Win with Roosevelt" painted on the side of her plane. She met with Franklin Roosevelt after his victory, spending most of their thirty minutes together urging him to include a woman in his cabinet. He did—Frances Perkins, secretary of labor, and the first woman to serve in the US cabinet.

At the same time, in Germany, Thea Rasche's flying life was disrupted by the violent rise of Adolf Hitler and the Nazi Party. The Nazis banned books Rasche had written about aviation, charging that they glorified American and English fliers. Rasche joined the Nazi Party in 1933—only, she would later insist, so she could keep her precious pilot's license. After World War II, she was put on trial in Germany for suspected Nazi activities. The court cleared her of the charges, finding that she had not used her flying skills to help Hitler's war effort.

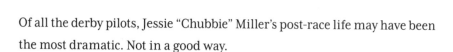

Of all the derby pilots, Jessie "Chubbie" Miller's post-race life may have been the most dramatic. Not in a good way.

Like many of the pilots, Miller struggled to make a living during the Depression. In 1932, she was living in Miami with Bill Lancaster, copilot of her famous 1928 flight from England to Australia. They were broke. On especially hungry nights, Bill would swipe a chicken from the neighbor's yard, and, since the power company had shut off their electricity, they'd cook the stolen bird on an outdoor fire.

Chubbie met a young writer, Haden Clarke, who suggested she could make some money by writing a memoir of her flying adventures. Haden offered to help with the project. Bill got jealous. The men had screaming fights. Late one night, Chubbie woke to the sound of a fist pounding on her bedroom door.

"An awful thing has happened!" Bill wailed. "Haden has shot himself!"

Haden was dead. The police came. They found suicide notes. They hauled both Bill and Chubbie to jail, questioning them for hours. Chubbie was released, but the cops were convinced Bill was not innocent. The gun that had killed Haden belonged to Bill. And, under grilling, Bill admitted to forging the suicide notes.

This whole scandal—including the sensational murder trial—made daily headlines from America to Australia, and has since been the subject of entire books. In short, the jury stunned most observers by acquitting Bill of murder. The mystery of Clarke's death remains unsolved.

Chubbie Miller settled in England, took a job managing an airport, and met and married a fellow pilot, John Pugh. Seeing war with Germany on the horizon, she suggested the formation of a corps of female pilots, an idea that blossomed into the Women's Section of the Air Transport Auxiliary.

During World War II, 166 women from ten countries—including derby contestant Edith Foltz—performed the vital job of ferrying fighter and bomber planes between bases for the Royal Air Force.

Missing the 1929 Women's Air Derby hardly hampered Elinor Smith's path to glory. After smashing a series of air records in 1930, Smith was voted by her fellow pilots, men and women, as the top female pilot of the year. Beating out Amelia Earhart—and especially her tireless promoter, George Putnam—was icing on the cake. She was still just nineteen.

Smith went on to have a long and illustrious career. She hosted radio

Elinor Smith was the first woman to be featured on a box of Wheaties.

shows about aviation and air races, and, in 1934, became the first woman to be featured on a box of Wheaties cereal. In 2000, eighty-eight and in need of new adventures, Smith got behind the controls of NASA's fiendishly challenging space shuttle flight simulator.

She landed the shuttle, no problem.

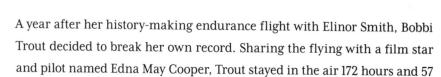

A year after her history-making endurance flight with Elinor Smith, Bobbi Trout decided to break her own record. Sharing the flying with a film star and pilot named Edna May Cooper, Trout stayed in the air 172 hours and 57 minutes, celebrating her twenty-fifth birthday with a chocolate cake lowered by rope from the refueling plane above.

"I hated like the deuce to have to come down," Bobbi said after finally being forced to the ground by an oil leak.

Bobbi went on to enjoy decades of adventures as a pilot, flight instructor, inventor, photographer, and more. She started a factory during World War II, using machines of her own design to recycle airplane parts for the military. In 1999, the 70th anniversary of the Women's Air Derby, Bobbi was honored as the last surviving racer. "When women did something in those days, it was quite extraordinary," she said, looking back on the trailblazing race. "People thought they were either crazy or doing something wonderful."

The women who came after Bobbi would argue for wonderful.

When Bobbi Trout died in 2003, at age ninety-seven, friends and fans gathered at an airport to toast her memory. Terri Lincoln, a helicopter pilot for the Los Angeles Police Department, spoke of the lasting influence of Trout and her pioneering generation of fliers. "Every woman before me has helped tremendously and been a tremendous inspiration in my life," Lincoln said. "As hard as it was for me, it was much harder for them."

"I believe in the independence of women," Ruth Elder said, "and experience has proved they can accomplish as great things as men."

Elder married Walter Camp after the derby. But if he really expected her to give up flying, as he'd publicly declared, he was in for a disappointment. The marriage lasted just three years.

Ruth's fame began to fade in the 1930s. She'd beaten the odds, gone from rags to riches, but she was not a gifted performer, and she knew it. After one stage show in New York, Elder said of the audience: "They were more terrifying than all the waves of the ocean, and I wanted to scream and run." Once called "Miss America of Aviation," Ruth lived a quiet life in San Francisco, running an aviation school and working in advertising. The one thing that never changed was her love of flying.

"There is nothing," she said, "like the whir of propellers and the glide of the machine through space to calm one's nerves and give one the feeling of absolute freedom."

Pancho Barnes watched her funds dwindle as the Depression dragged on. No longer able to afford her lavish Los Angeles lifestyle, Pancho sold her beloved Mystery Ship, moved to a ranch in the Mohave Desert, and opened a dusty saloon with horses, a swimming pool, and its own landing strip.

Pancho's Fly Inn—or, as it came to be known, The Happy Bottom Riding Club—became a favorite place for test pilots from nearby Edwards Air Force Base to blow off steam. Pancho loved swapping flying stories with young guns from the base and promised a free steak dinner to the first pilot to break the speed of sound, 767 miles per hour. She proudly served the steak to Chuck Yeager when he did it in a rocket-powered Bell X-1 in 1947.

Well into her sixties, Pancho Barnes was still flying planes, wearing men's jeans, banging out songs at the piano, and living by her own rules. Pancho's

Pancho Barnes surrounded by fellow pilots, including Chuck Yeager (to her left), at her Happy Bottom Riding Club.

advice on life: "Don't even try to be like anybody else, because we've seen it already. Be yourself!"

MARVEL CROSSON'S KID BROTHER FLIES ON

That was the headline of an article about Joe Crosson four months after the derby. Joe was devastated by the death of his sister, but, like Marvel, flying was his life. He returned to Alaska and went back to work.

"Why shouldn't Joe go back to his work?" his mother said. "Aviation is his job, just as attending the sick is a doctor's mission in life. Marvel died just as she wanted to go—in an airplane. There are dangers, of course, but the children must lead their own lives."

Joe became a legendary Alaskan bush pilot, flying medicine through blizzards, landing on patches of ice, saving communities cut off from help. Joe and his wife, Lillian, named their daughter Sue Marvel Crosson.

What about the rumors of sabotage? Had someone tampered with Marvel's plane—or *any* of the planes—during the Women's Air Derby? If Joe Crosson had an opinion, he never shared it publicly.

But many of the racers remained convinced that there had been a calculated campaign to sabotage the race.

"*Something* happened," Bobbi Trout said years after the derby. "We thought someone was up to something." She was especially suspicious about that first night in San Bernardino. "Some people saw a group of mechanics fooling around among our planes that night."

Pancho Barnes agreed. "There was a lot of dirty work going on, and many planes were tampered with," she said. Forty years after the race, Pancho added an explosive detail: "There was a lot of sabotage in that race because one of the women's husbands felt the easy way for her to win the race was to put all the other ships out."

She never named the husband.

The "beware of sabotage" telegram sent to Thea Rasche from New York City was never explained.

We'll never know exactly what happened. Planes were unreliable in 1929. There were accidents in every cross-country race. The derby pilots knew this, though, and *they* found all the mishaps suspicious.

What we can say for sure is that if anyone *did* set out to destroy the Women's Air Derby, the effort was a total failure. The women set out to prove they could fly as well as men, and they proved it. There was no turning back.

On September 4, 1936, at Mines Field in Los Angeles, sixty thousand fans scanned the sky for incoming airplanes. They'd come to see the finish of the Bendix Transcontinental Speed Race, the world's most prestigious cross-country air race.

For years, for all the usual reasons, women had been banned. This year, thanks to pressure from Amelia Earhart and others, several two-pilot female teams were in the running. Convinced the women couldn't keep up with the men, the race sponsor, Vincent Bendix, added a $2,500 prize for the first female team to finish.

It was a consolation prize. The *real* winners would get $4,500.

Planes were already much faster than they'd been in the 1920s, and cross-country races were now one-day affairs. The teams had taken off from New York City before dawn that morning, with several planned stops on the way to California. All day, news came into Los Angeles about storms along the route, forced landings in fields, bailouts from flaming planes.

Finally, just after 5:00 PM, fourteen hours and fifty-five minutes after the start of the race, an electric blue Beech Staggerwing sped in from the east and screamed over the finish line. Fans shouted:

"It's Louise Thaden!"

Crowds rushed the plane as it taxied to a stop. Thaden and her copilot, Blanche Noyes, looked out from the cockpit, confused by the excitement. They'd been battling headwinds all day. They knew the men's teams had faster planes. So why were people hopping up and down?

Blanche and Louise jumped to the ground. People started grabbing their hands, clapping their backs, shoving papers to sign in their faces. It was like the finish line in Cleveland in 1929 all over again. But why?

"We think you've won," a man said.

Louise grumbled, "This is no time for joking."

Everyone kept insisting they were the first team to reach Los Angeles. The judges made it official: Louise Thaden and Blanche Noyes had won the Bendix. Thaden thought that Mr. Bendix looked a tad disappointed as he handed her *both* prizes—the "consolation prize" and the big first-place trophy.

Beating the top male pilots was another first for Louise Thaden, another blast to the wall facing women pilots. "Through the immediate years ahead," she wrote in her 1938 flying memoir, *High, Wide, and Frightened*, "let us hope the wall will, from disuse, crumble away."

It has crumbled. Gradually.

Inspired by the success of the Women's Air Derby, the number of female pilots in the United States doubled in the three months after the race, and it has climbed steadily from there. During World War II, women of the WASPs—the Women Airforce Service Pilots—served as test pilots and instructors and ferried planes between bases. In 1953, Jacqueline Cochran, who led the WASPs during the war, became the first female flier to break the sound barrier. In 1993, the US Department of Defense lifted its long-standing ban on women flying combat missions.

On June 18, 1983, physicist and astronaut Sally Ride orbited Earth aboard the space shuttle *Challenger*, making history as the first American woman in space. The reaction to Ride's courage and skill would have felt familiar to the pilots of the Women's Air Derby—millions were moved and inspired; some wanted to turn back the clock. One late-night talk show host "joked" that the *Challenger* flight had been delayed while Ride looked for a purse to match her shoes.

"It's too bad this is such a big deal," Ride told reporters. "It's too bad our society isn't further along."

Still, Sally Ride and the female fliers and astronauts who followed had come a long way. And they knew who had paved the path. In 1991, American astronaut Linda Godwin carried Louise Thaden's flying helmet into space. In 1995, when Eileen Collins became the first woman to pilot the space shuttle, she took along Bobbi Trout's pilot's license.

In her own long lifetime in aviation, Louise Thaden set several more speed and endurance records, ran a flying school, and worked for the Bureau of Air Commerce (now the Federal Aviation Administration), making airports safer. And she accomplished her goal of having both career and family. She and Herb raised two children, Bill and Pat. Louise took them each for their first flight when they were three months old, and they both became pilots.

Louise Thaden never spoke much about her own accomplishments, and it wasn't until Pat was old enough to start dating that she realized what a big

Eileen Collins

Jacqueline Cochran

Linda Godwin

Sally Ride

deal her mother was. What tipped her off was that boys kept coming to the house early to talk to her famous mom.

In 1960, when she was fifty-five, Louise got to copilot an Air Force T-33 jet with her son, Lieutenant Bill Thaden. As they soared past twenty-one thousand feet, Bill joked over the intercom that they'd just passed her altitude record from 1928.

When she finally retired from flying in 1974, sixty-two years after leaping from a barn roof with an open umbrella, Louise Thaden was asked about the proudest moment of her history-making career. Her blue eyes twinkled. She said, without a doubt, it was winning the Women's Air Derby of 1929.

So why is Amelia Earhart the one name everyone knows?

She deserves the love, but so does Louise Thaden. So do Marvel Crosson, Pancho Barnes, Elinor Smith, and so many more. Why is Amelia Earhart the one who kids (including my daughter when she was nine, helping to inspire this book) dress up as for Halloween?

Early inspiration: Anna as Amelia Earhart, two years before I started researching the Women's Air Derby.

It's partly because of her two history-making Atlantic flights. It's partly thanks to the nonstop marketing of her publisher and, eventually, her husband, George Putnam. It's partly because she was so smart and passionate, so tireless in promoting opportunities for women, and so inspiring to others—ever since hitching that ride to Kinner Field, when the girl in the back seat gaped with wonder at a real-life flier, Amelia Earhart's adventurous spirit has fueled generations of dreams. But the biggest factor in Earhart's lasting fame is her mysterious disappearance.

Her plan was to fly around the world. No pilot, man or woman, had ever circumnavigated the globe along the equator, a route that would zigzag twenty-nine thousand miles across continents and oceans.

"I have a feeling that there is just about one more good flight left in my system, and I hope this is it," she said before setting out. "Anyway, when I have finished this job, I mean to give up major long-distance flights."

On May 21, 1937, Amelia Earhart took off from Oakland, California, in a twin-engine Lockheed Electra with her navigator, Fred Noonan. After stops in South America, Africa, Asia, and Australia, they reached Lae, New Guinea, by the end of June. With seven thousand miles to go, the most dangerous leg of the flight—over the world's largest ocean—lay ahead.

Earhart and Noonan left New Guinea on July 2 with plenty of fuel to reach their destination, tiny Howland Island in the South Pacific. The 2,556-mile flight should have taken about eighteen hours. A US Coast Guard ship, the *Itasca*, waited off the Howland coast to help guide Earhart's plane in.

"We must be on you but cannot see you," Earhart radioed to the *Itasca* an hour after they were due in Howland. "But gas is running low."

Sixteen minutes later, her voice was heard again. "We are circling but cannot see island, cannot hear you."

There was one more garbled message. Then, nothing.

The search for Amelia Earhart began the next morning. It has never ended.

For weeks after the disappearance, navy planes circled vast stretches of the Pacific Ocean around Howland. No trace of Earhart or her plane was found. In the years since, researchers and historians have proposed a series of competing theories about what happened.

One theory is that Earhart managed to put the plane down on a tiny coral island. She and Noonan survived the landing but later died of hunger or thirst. Another guess is that they landed in the Marshall Islands, which were then controlled by Japan. The tensions that would eventually lead to war between Japan and the United States were already rising, and Japanese authorities, according to this theory, suspected the American fliers of being spies. Earhart and Noonan were imprisoned and executed, the theory goes. Or possibly shipped back to the United States under false names.

The least exciting—and by far the most likely—explanation is that Amelia Earhart's plane ran out of fuel and crashed into the ocean. It's what her fellow pilots believed.

"I believe she went down at sea," decided Neta Snook, Earhart's first flight instructor, after studying the case for years.

Ruth Nichols came to the same conclusion. "Amelia flew on across the trackless Pacific until her last drop of fuel was gone and then sank quickly and cleanly into the deep blue sea."

Louise Thaden saw Amelia Earhart for the last time in January 1937 at an airport in Burbank, California. Both pilots had just landed. Louise taxied up to Earhart's Electra and shouted:

"Would you please give me your autograph, Miss Earhart?"

Amelia looked over. She saw who it was and smiled. They both got out of their planes. Earhart was instantly surrounded by fans. As always, she took the time to chat and sign autographs.

When Louise worked her way up, Amelia told the crowd, "You know Louise Thaden, don't you? You should have *her* autograph."

So they both signed for a while. Then they walked into a hangar and sat on the edge of an inflated rubber life raft.

"You've gone crazy on me," Thaden would later remember telling Earhart. "Why stick your neck out a mile on this round-the-world flight? You don't need to do anything more."

That made Amelia Earhart laugh. "Listen, *you* can't talk to *me* about taking chances!"

Fair point, Louise conceded. "But just the same," she said, "I wish you wouldn't do it."

They sat for a minute without talking. The only sounds came from airplane engines out on the field.

"If I bop off, you can carry on," Amelia said, "you can all carry on." Smiling, she added, "But I'll be back."

They walked together to Amelia's car. Louise still had so much to say. And, really, nothing to say. They understood each other without words.

The pilots shook hands. Amelia Earhart got into her car and drove away.

"Eternal life, I think, is a life so lived that its deeds carry on through the ages," Louise Thaden would write two years later, after Earhart's disappearance. "A.E. has carved a niche too deep to ever be forgotten. She will live."

Thaden was right. It's been over eighty years, and Amelia Earhart lives. So does Louise Thaden. So do Bobbi Trout and Ruth Elder, Pancho Barnes and Marvel Crosson. So do all the pilots of the Women's Air Derby.

They started by jumping off roofs. They wound up kicking down doors—for themselves, and everyone else.

SOURCE NOTES

My research for this book began with two excellent sources: Heather Taylor's documentary *Breaking Through the Clouds* and Gene Nora Jessen's book *The Powder Puff Derby of 1929*. I also relied on the pilots' own accounts of their flying adventures, in particular Louise Thaden's *High, Wide, and Frightened* and *So They Flew*, Marvel Crosson's article "How I Learned to Fly," Amelia Earhart's *20 Hrs. 40 Min* and *The Fun of It*, Elinor Smith's *Aviatrix*, Ruth Elder's articles in the *Minneapolis Star Tribune*, Ruth Nichols's *Wings for Life*, and the series of articles about Pancho Barnes in *Hi-Desert Spectator*, which are based on interviews with Pancho. The Bobbi Trout biography *Just Plane Crazy*, Muriel Earhart Morrissey's *Amelia, My Courageous Sister*, and Lorraine O'Donnell Doyle's *Second to None* all reprint pilots' letters, original documents, and hundreds of article clippings.

The Women's Air Derby was on the front pages of newspapers all over the country every day of the race. Papers in cities along the route (marked with an asterisk in the list on page 258) were especially valuable, since they sent reporters to talk with the pilots and report on events firsthand. Newspapers were also very useful in researching the pilots' record-setting flights and crashes—both were big news in the 1920s.

BORN TO FLY

1 Louise Thaden tells the umbrella story and of always wanting to fly: Thaden, *High, Wide, and Frightened*, 9; her children recall the tale: Thaden, "Louise Thaden: Pioneer Aviator," *Vintage Airplane*, April 1989, 20–25.

1 Ruth Elder tells of her horse leap: "Ruth Elder Dared Perils of Ocean Hop to Escape Drab Poverty, She Writes," *Minneapolis Star Tribune*, June 17, 1928.

3 Marvel Crosson describes her canceled flight: Crosson, "How I Learned to Fly," *The Country Gentleman*, September 1929, 26.

3 Amelia Earhart's sister, "Pidge," tells the roller-coaster story: Morrissey, *Amelia, My Courageous Sister*, 16–17.

4 Air racing in the 1920s: Gwynn-Jones, *The Air Racers*, 139–178; Walker, *Powder Puff Derby*, 2–3.

4 Ruth Elder wanted to play football: "Young Anniston Aviatrix as Girl Liked Fun and Feared Nothing," *Anniston (AL) Star*, October 20, 1927.

4 Marvel and Joe take apart their dad's car: Crosson, "How I Learned to Fly," *The Country Gentleman*, September 1929, 26.

5 "It's not so awful big": Mattison, "A Girl Flies to Fame," *Pacific Flyer*, April 1929, 6.

5 Amelia's sled and "You don't realize": Earhart, *The Fun of It*, 11–12.

6 "Some elders have to be shocked": Earhart, *The Fun of It*, 11.

6 "Poor Dobbins": Schultz, *Pancho*, 17; childhood stories also found in Kessler, *The Happy Bottom Riding Club*, 15–17; Mitchell, "Pancho Barnes: A Legend in Our Lifetime: Part 1 of 4," *Hi-Desert Spectator*, Jan-Feb 1963, 7–9, 30–31.

6 Bobbi Trout seeing her first plane and Aunt Edna's reaction: Veca, *Just Plane Crazy*, 8–9.

6, 8 Earhart collecting articles about interesting careers: Morrissey, *Amelia, My Courageous Sister*, 48.

8 "In those days": Crosson, "How I Learned to Fly," *The Country Gentleman*, September 1929, 26.

RACING TO THE SKY

9–10 Marvel background and San Diego trip: Crosson, "How I Learned to Fly," *The Country Gentleman*, September 1929, 26; Mondor, "The Short, Brilliant Career of Alaska's First Woman Pilot," *Anchorage Daily News*, June 19, 2016.

9 "There were planes everywhere": Tordoff, *Mercy Pilot*, 16.

10 "We've only got two-fifty" conversation, first flight, and reaction: Crosson, "How I Learned to Fly," *The Country Gentleman*, September 1929, 26.

11 Marvel and Joe buy a plane: Crosson, "How I Learned to Fly," *The Country Gentleman*, September 1929, 96; Tordoff, *Mercy Pilot*, 17–18.

11 "When Mother and Father saw" and "Well, if anything is going to happen": Crosson, "How I Learned to Fly," *The Country Gentleman*, September 1929, 96.

11–12 Amelia Earhart background: Earhart, *The Fun of It*, 19–20.

12 "I did not understand it at the time": Earhart, *Last Flight*, 3.

13 Neta Snook recalls meeting Amelia Earhart, including "Do not touch the controls": Snook, *I Taught Amelia to Fly*, 1–2.

13 "I see you are busy" and responses: Snook, *I Taught Amelia to Fly*, 1–2.

13 "My parents aren't in accord": Snook, *I Taught Amelia to Fly*, 2.

13–15 Background on early female pilots: Lebow, *Before Amelia*, 1–14, 131–145; Adams, *Heroines of the Sky*, 3–26; Jaros, *Heroes Without Legacy*, 9–26; "Miss Quimby and W.A.P. Willard Killed in Fall," *Boston Globe*, July 2, 1912.

15 "It would be well": Lebow, *Before Amelia*, 6.

15 "You really weren't serious": Earhart, *The Fun of It*, 25.

15 "We gave up everything": Crosson, "How I Learned to Fly," *The Country Gentleman*, September 1929, 96.

15 For a photo and description of a Curtiss N-9, see the Smithsonian National Air and Space Museum website: airandspace.si.edu/collection-objects/curtiss-n-9h.

16 "We were proud of it": Crosson, "How I Learned to Fly," *The Country Gentleman*, September 1929, 96.

16 "Never mind, sister" and Louise's response: Mattison, "A Girl Flies to Fame," *Pacific Flyer*, April 1929, 5.

16–17 Louise Thaden describes her time in Wichita and being scolded by her boss: Thaden, *High, Wide, and Frightened*, 12.

17 "How'd you like to go to California": Thaden, *High, Wide, and Frightened*, 12; Thaden, "Breaking Records in the Clouds," *St. Louis Post-Dispatch*, June 11, 1930.

17 "I'm going to California!" and family reaction: Thaden, *High, Wide, and Frightened*, 12–13.

20 "Boy, did that ruin my feelings": "Pioneer of Flight Lends Expo an Air of History," *Los Angeles Times*, July 11, 1999.

20 "I could do that!" and details of gas station story: Veca, *Just Plane Crazy*, 13; mansplaining incident: Veca, *Just Plane Crazy*, 21.

GOLDEN AGE

21–23 "You may not live to a ripe, old age" and details of Trout's first lesson: Veca, *Just Plane Crazy*, 26–29.

23–25 Earhart describes her early lessons with Neta Snook: Earhart, *The Fun of It*, 31–33.

25 "I know, I guess I was daydreaming": Snook, *I Taught Amelia to Fly*, 122.

25 "Do you know anyone" and the story of buying and testing the airplane motor: Crosson, "How I Learned to Fly," *The Country Gentleman*, September 1929, 96, 98; Tordoff, *Mercy Pilot*, 18.

28 Physics of flight: The Smithsonian National Air and Space Museum in Washington, DC, has an amazing, hands-on "Four Forces" display; a lot of the components are viewable online at the Smithsonian's "How Things Fly" website.

29 "It flies!": Crosson, "How I Learned to Fly," *The Country Gentleman*, September 1929, 98.

29 "Those good fellows," Marvel's early lessons, and parents' reaction: Crosson, "How I Learned to Fly," *The Country Gentleman*, September 1929, 98; Tordoff, *Mercy Pilot*, 22–23.

30–32 Pancho's teen years: Kessler, *The Happy Bottom Riding Club*, 20–30; Mitchell, "Pancho Barnes: A Legend in Our Lifetime: Part 1 of 4," *Hi-Desert Spectator*, Jan-Feb 1963, 30–31.

30 "I was no man's maid servant": Mitchell, "Pancho Barnes: A Legend in Our Lifetime: Part 4 of 4," *Hi-Desert Spectator*, May-June 1963, 17.

30 "I think you'll pass as a guy," Mexico adventure, and nickname origin: Mitchell, "Pancho Barnes: A Legend in Our Lifetime: Part 2 of 4," *Hi-Desert Spectator*, March 1963, 6–7.

32 "Everyone will be flying airplanes": Kessler, *The Happy Bottom Riding Club*, 5.

32 "When is it you wanted to start" and details of this flight: Kessler, *The Happy Bottom Riding Club*, 48–50; Mitchell, "Pancho Barnes: A Legend in Our Lifetime: Part 3 of 4," *Hi-Desert Spectator*, April 1963, 5–6.

DREAMS AND NIGHTMARES

33 Pancho's close call: Mitchell, "Pancho Barnes: A Legend in Our Lifetime: Part 3 of 4," *Hi-Desert Spectator*, April 1963, 10.

34 Marvel's motor dies over the ocean: "She'll Join Her Brother as Pilot on Alaska Air Line," *Manitowoc (WI) Herald Times*, June 10, 1927.

34–35 Amelia Earhart's first crash: Earhart, *20 Hrs. 40 Min*, 31; Snook, *I Taught Amelia to Fly*, 126.

35, 37 Trout's crash and mother's reaction: Veca, *Just Plane Crazy*, 31–34; Veca also reprints several clippings about the crash from Los Angeles papers, March 16, 1928.

37 "They never get anything right" and returning to work and flight: Veca, *Just Plane Crazy*, 36, 38.

38 Earhart's boring job: Earhart, *20 Hrs. 40 Min*, 23; Earhart, *The Fun of It*, 25.

38 "But you don't look like an aviatrix": Earhart, *The Fun of It*, 26.

38 "It was very odd": Earhart, *The Fun of It*, 26.

39 "The only time a lady's name": Lovell, *The Sound of Wings*, 43.

39–40 Background on women in the Roaring Twenties, flappers: Collins, *American Women*, 327–349; Dumenil, *Modern Temper*, 112–113.

39 "Haircuts cost at least a dollar": Crosson, "How I Learned to Fly," *The Country Gentleman*, September 1929, 26.

40 Bessie Coleman biographical information: the official Bessie Coleman website, bessiecoleman.org, the PBS "American Experience Fly Girls" website, and the National Aviation Hall of Fame's site.

41 Thaden's life in Oakland: Thaden, *High, Wide, and Frightened*, 14; Thaden's job selling planes was so unusual she was featured in many articles, including: "Plane Salesgirl Dates Career from Barn 'Hop'" *San Francisco Call*, December 7, 1927; "Beautiful Wichita Girl Flies! And How! Sells Travel Airs," *Wichita Eagle*, December 31, 1927.

42 "tall, blonde, attractive" and the story of meeting Herb Thaden and their first flight together: Thaden, *High, Wide, and Frightened*, 14–15.

42 Ruth Elder describes her miserable life: "Ruth Elder Tells of Her Struggles After Marriage," *Minneapolis Star Tribune*, June 18, 1928.

43 "When I passed my solo": "Family Thought Her Insane; Haldeman Believed Flying Plan Fad, Says Ruth Elder," *Minneapolis Star Tribune*, June 19, 1928.

43 Racing to cross the Atlantic in 1927: This subject has inspired entire books, including Jackson, *Atlantic Fever*, and Hamlen, *Flight Fever*.

43 "I'm going to fly across the Atlantic": "The American Super-Girl and Her Critics," *The Literary Digest*, October 29, 1927, 55.

43 "Girl, are you crazy?": "Ruth Elder: From Beauty Contestant to Heroine," *Anniston (AL) Star*, July 4, 1976.

44 "I know that it's a long chance": "The American Super-Girl and Her Critics," *The Literary Digest*, October 29, 1927, 55.

RACING ACROSS THE ATLANTIC

45 "What will you wear on the flight" and following questions and answers: "Ruth Elder All Ready at L.I. Field for Sea Hop," *Brooklyn Daily Eagle*, September 13, 1927.

48 "Girl Flyer's Mother Is Near Collapse": headline of small article in *Anniston (AL) Star*, October 13, 1927.

48 For the details of Ruth Elder's Atlantic attempt: Brooks-Pazmany, *United States Women*

in Aviation, 1919–1929, 21–22; "The American Girl," *Aero Digest*, November 1927, 515, 612; "Ruth Determined," *Pittsburgh Press*, September 15, 1927; "Ruth Elder Is Yet Unreported," *Anniston (AL) Star*, October 12, 1927; "Anxious Elder Family Waits for News of Ruth," *Anniston (AL) Star*, October 12, 1927; "Ruth Elder Fourth Woman to Seek Fame as First Ocean Flyer," *Chicago Tribune*, October 13, 1927; "Ruth Elder's Heroism Told After Landing" *Detroit Free Press*, October 16, 1927.

48 "Fine!" and "The old motor": "Ruth Elder Tells of Atlantic Flight," *Anniston (AL) Star*, October 19, 1927.

48–49 Elder describes the sea landing and rescue: "Ruth Elder Saved Because Boat Was Delayed, Is Feted," *Minneapolis Star Tribune*, June 20, 1928.

49 "Ruth is a mighty smart girl" and other Elder family reactions: "Ruth Elder Is Heroine to Younger Brothers in Anniston," *Anniston (AL) Star*, October 19, 1927.

49 Negative reactions to Elder's flight, including newspaper quotes: "The American Super-Girl and Her Critics," *The Literary Digest*, October 29, 1927, 52–55.

50 Elder discusses reaction to the flight: "Ruth Elder: From Beauty Contestant to Heroine," *Anniston (AL) Star*, July 4, 1976.

51 "I expect to try another:" "Ruth Elder Exhausted by Ceremonies," *Anniston (AL) Star*, October 20, 1927.

51 Putnam and Railey's decision to offer Atlantic flight to Amelia Earhart: Railey, *Touch'd with Madness*, 100–101; Morrissey, *Amelia, My Courageous Sister*, 78–79; Lovell, *The Sound of Wings*, 92–93.

51 "Phone for you, Miss Earhart!" and phone conversation with Railey: Earhart, *The Fun of It*, 58–59.

52 "I might as well lay the cards" and Earhart's response: Earhart, *The Fun of It*, 59.

52 "How could I refuse": Morrissey, *Amelia, My Courageous Sister*, 78.

53 "If they liked me too well": Putnam, *Wide Margins*, 295.

53 Earhart describes the flight preparations: Earhart, *20 Hrs. 40 Min*, 39–50; Earhart, *The Fun of It*, 61–66; Lovell, *The Sound of Wings*, 103–117.

53 "Dear Dad": Morrissey, *Amelia, My Courageous Sister*, 79.

54 "Girl Pilot Dares the Atlantic": Amelia's sister, Muriel, describes seeing this article and family reaction: Morrissey, *Amelia, My Courageous Sister*, 81–82.

54 "Where is Miss Earhart now?": Earhart, *20 Hrs. 40 Min*, introduction by Marion Perkins, Earhart's boss at Denison House.

54–55 Earhart's recollections of the flight: Earhart, *20 Hrs. 40 Min*, 91–112; Earhart, *The Fun of It*, 69–81.

54 "The sun is sinking" and "The highest peaks": Earhart, *20 Hrs. 40 Min*, 100.

55 "Where are we?": Earhart, *20 Hrs. 40 Min*, 109.

55 "We all favored sticking": Earhart, *20 Hrs. 40 Min*, 109.

55 "We could see only a few miles": Earhart, *20 Hrs. 40 Min*, 110.

56 Earhart's final log entry: Morrissey, *Amelia, My Courageous Sister*, 86.

PUSHING LIMITS

57 "I'll get a boat": Earhart, *The Fun of It*, 81.

57–59 Massive response to Earhart's flight: Morrissey, *Amelia, My Courageous Sister*, 95–101; Lovell, *The Sound of Wings*, 126–130.

58 *McCall's* job, "Cigarette smoking is to be expected," and "I suppose you drink": Morrissey, *Amelia, My Courageous Sister*, 101; Backus, *Letters from Amelia*, 81.

59 "What's the matter?" and Earhart's response: Burke, *Winged Legend*, 97.

59 Pancho Barnes flies over the church: Schultz, *Pancho*, 60.

59 Pancho describes early flying adventures and her love of "cannibal sandwiches": Tate, *The Lady Who Tamed Pegasus*, 32–36; Kessler, *The Happy Bottom Riding Club*, 56–60.

61 "We swaggered a bit": Tate, *The Lady Who Tamed Pegasus*, 32.

61 "I don't give a darn about saving": Schultz, *Pancho*, 66.

61–63 Marvel Crosson describes her life in Alaska in a series of unpublished letters, used courtesy of Sue Crosson Fraser; more details in Mondor, "The Short, Brilliant Career of Alaska's First Woman Pilot," *Anchorage Daily News*, June 19, 2016.

61 "It takes hours to get": Marvel Crosson letter to former teacher Ms. Hagen, February 18, 1928.

62 "Even Joe admits": "All About Alaska's Airplane Grocery Girl," *Minneapolis Star Tribune*, July 17, 1927.

63 "Well, Miss Hagen": Marvel Crosson letter to former teacher Ms. Hagen, April 14, 1927.

63 Married women statistics and Ford quote: Collins, *American Women*, 349.

64 Thaden describes her transport test: Thaden, *High, Wide, and Frightened*, 35–36.

64 "Clothed in my newborn conceit": Thaden, *High, Wide, and Frightened*, 25.

65 Thaden recalls her crash and recovery: Thaden, *High, Wide, and Frightened*, 26–27;

crash covered in local press: "Oakland Flier Killed in Crash," *Oakland Tribune*, August 20, 1928; "S.F. Bride Hurt with Aviator in Alameda Crash," *San Francisco Chronicle*, August 20, 1928.

65 "The plane is a complete washout": Thaden, *High, Wide, and Frightened*, 27.

65 "There was an ache in my heart": Thaden, *High, Wide, and Frightened*, 27.

66 "A pilot who says": Thaden, *High, Wide, and Frightened*, 5.

66–68 Thaden's altitude record flight, including conversation about oxygen with doctor: Thaden, *High, Wide, and Frightened*, 19–24.

RACING FOR RECORDS

70 "I can establish a higher altitude": "Aviatrix Sets World Record," *Oakland Tribune*, December 8, 1928.

70 "Once I make up my mind": Veca, *Just Plane Crazy*, 51.

70 Bobbi Trout's record flight: "Remains in Air Twelve Hours Alone," *Santa Ana Register*, January 3, 1929; "Record Set by Girl Flyer," *Los Angeles Times*, January 4, 1929.

70 "You did it!": Veca, *Just Plane Crazy*, 53; the authors, who knew Bobbi Trout, reprint many article clippings from this and other notable Trout flights.

70–71 "I always hated working around the house": "Remains in Air Twelve Hours Alone," *Santa Ana Register*, January 3, 1929.

71 "In an age when girls": Smith, *Aviatrix*, preface, vii.

71 Elinor Smith recalls her famous bridge stunt: Smith, *Aviatrix*, 3–15; "Says She Flew Under East River Bridges," *New York Times*, October 22, 1928.

71 "You remember—we sent for her" and conversation with Mayor Walker: Smith, *Aviatrix*, 18.

73 Smith's endurance record flight: "Elinor Smith Had to Sing 5 Hours to Keep Awake in Night Endurance Flight," *Brooklyn Daily Eagle*, January 31, 1929.

73 "It pleased me": Smith, *Aviatrix*, 89.

73 "Gosh, I hate to take the record" and "Tomboy Stays in Air 17 Hours to Avoid Washing Dishes" headline: Veca, *Just Plane Crazy*, 68.

73 Trout retakes the endurance record: "Bobbi Trout Sets up New Flying Marks," *Santa Maria (CA) Times*, February 11, 1929.

73 Thaden's endurance flight: "Wichita Girl Captures Second Air Mark," *Wichita Eagle*, March 18, 1929.

73 Smith retakes the record: "Elinor Smith, 17, Sets Record in 26-Hour Flight," *New York Daily News*, April 25, 1929; "Flying Flapper Breaks Record," *Poughkeepsie (NY) Eagle-News*, April 25, 1929.

74 "I hope Bobbi will set": "Flyer's Sister Plans to Try for Altitude Mark," *Los Angeles Times*, February 7, 1929.

74–75 Marvel Crosson's altitude record and "Gee, it was cold up there": "24,000 Foot Altitude Record for Women Believed Fixed by Miss Crosson," *Los Angeles Times*, May 29, 1929.

75 "I climbed the ship": "San Diego Girl Given Official Altitude Record," *San Diego Union*, June 20, 1929.

75 "New Star of the Clouds": Tordoff, *Mercy Pilot*, 95.

75 "Why don't you stop flying?" and Marvel's response: Crosson, "How I Learned to Fly," *The Country Gentleman*, September 1929, 26.

75 "A long-distance flyer": "Hawaii Flight Hero Denies Engagement," *Santa Monica (CA) Outlook*, June 3, 1929.

76 "I want to race": Sumner, *Women Pilots of Alaska*, 11.

THE WOMEN'S AIR DERBY

77 For background on long-distance air racing: Gwynn-Jones, *The Air Racers*, 23–28, 66–80; Naughton, "The Birdmen at Belmont Park," *American Heritage*, April 1956; "The Disastrous Race" *London Daily News*, June 19, 1911.

78 "A man can damage a plane": Earhart, *The Fun of It*, 137.

78 The story behind the derby and Elizabeth McQueen's role: Taylor, *Breaking Through the Clouds*; more background in Gwynn-Jones, *The Air Racers*, 180–181; Spicer, *The Flying Adventures of Jessie Keith "Chubbie" Miller*, 97–98.

78–79 "Women are by nature": Gould, "Milady Takes the Air," *North American Review*, December 1929, 691; "Women pilots are too emotional": Jessen, *The Powder Puff Derby of 1929*, 59.

79 "The public press generally censured": McQueen wrote this on the first page of an undated report entitled "Women's International Association of Aeronautics," found in the Ninety-Nines Museum archives, Oklahoma City, OK.

79 Racers sign up for derby: "Marvel Crosson First Air Derby Entrant," *Santa Monica (CA) Outlook*, July 20, 1929; Taylor, *Breaking Through the Clouds*; Thaden, *High, Wide, and Frightened*, 37–38; Butler, *East to the Dawn*, 229.

81 "I know many boys": Earhart, *The Fun of It*, 143.

81 "I spent most of my childhood" and Ruth Nichols's childhood stories: Nichols, *Wings for Life*, 15–20.

82 "I was free as the air": Nichols, *Wings for Life*, 16.

83 "I came home grease-smeared": Nichols, *Wings for Life*, 36.

83 "Happy New Year, kid!" and Miami flight: Nichols, *Wings for Life*, 42–46; "New York–Miami Non-Stop Flight Made Yesterday," *Fort Lauderdale (FL) News*, January 5, 1928.

83 "Society's Flying Beauty" and other nicknames: Nichols, *Wings for Life*, 50.

83 "some high-pressure telephoning": Nichols, *Wings for Life*, 78.

84 "What is your ambition" and Smith's response: Lovell, *The Sound of Wings*, 140.

84 "You know, Elinor": Smith, *Aviatrix*, 100–101.

85 Race organizers consider adding male "navigators": Butler, *East to the Dawn*, 228; Taylor, *Breaking Through the Clouds*.

85 "This is just what we *don't* want": "Women Fliers Balk at Easy $10,000 Race," *New York Times*, June 12, 1929.

86 "There was absolutely no way": Smith, *Aviatrix*, 133.

87 Thaden describes waiting for her plane: Thaden, *High, Wide, and Frightened*, 43.

87 "If you girls don't keep out": Thaden, *High, Wide, and Frightened*, 43.

88 Marvel "delighted" with her plane: A reporter writing about Marvel's crash visited the Travel Air factory and included prerace details in the article, "Marvel Crosson Dies in Crash," *Wichita Beacon*, August 20, 1929; Thaden describes seeing the test flight: Thaden, *High, Wide, and Frightened*, 43.

88 Thaden describes her trip home and reception: Thaden, *High, Wide, and Frightened*, 39–41.

WHY WE FLY

90 Pilots flying course before race: "Women in Air Derby Here on Way to Coast," *Fort Worth Star-Telegram*, August 15, 1929.

90 "Miss Crosson is absorbing": "Quintet of New Entries Line Up for Women's Air Derby," *Santa Monica (CA) Outlook*, August 4, 1929.

90–92 "Why do you fly?": These questions and answers are from the remarkable article "Why Do Women Fly? They Speak for Themselves!" *Santa Monica (CA) Outlook*, August 11, 1929.

92 "Every flight has its thrills": Thaden, "Breaking Records in the Clouds," *St. Louis Post-Dispatch*, June 11, 1930.

92 "Think you can fly this ship" and Thaden's answer: Thaden, *High, Wide, and Frightened*, 44.

93–94 Thaden describes nearly dying from carbon monoxide poisoning on the way to the derby: Thaden, *High, Wide, and Frightened*, 44–45.

94–95 Race details: Jessen, *The Powder Puff Derby of 1929*, 63; Brooks-Pazmany, *United States Women in Aviation, 1919–1929*, 34–44; "Feminine Air Racers Ready for Start," *Santa Monica (CA) Outlook*, August 18, 1929; "San Diego Girl Will Lead Air Derby," *San Diego Union*, August 18, 1929.

95 "They came out with serious looks": "Girl Air Derby to Start Today," *Los Angeles Times*, August 18, 1929.

95 "If the twenty of us": "Thousands to Greet Famous Women Pilots," *San Bernardino Sun*, August 18, 1929.

95 "Give 'em heck, kid!" and Ruth Nichols's difficult trip to California: Nichols, *Wings for Life*, 79–90; "Woman Entrant in Air Derby Forced Down in Arizona," *Albuquerque Journal*, August 16, 1929.

96–97 Many papers printed maps of the route of the derby, including "Route of National Women's Air Derby," *Santa Monica (CA) Outlook*, August 16, 1929.

98 "There's an airplane down": Jessen, *The Powder Puff Derby of 1929*, 23.

100 "I've been flying around": Jessen, *The Powder Puff Derby of 1929*, 23.

100–101 Prerace banquet details: Jessen, *The Powder Puff Derby of 1929*, 37; "Women Fliers to Be Heavily Feted," *Santa Monica (CA) Outlook*, August 13, 1929; "Famed Flier Group Guests of Occasion," *Santa Monica (CA) Outlook*, August 14, 1929; Spicer, *The Flying Adventures of Jessie Keith "Chubbie" Miller*, 100.

101 "Beware of sabotage" telegram: Thaden, *High, Wide, and Frightened*, 46; Jessen, *The Powder Puff Derby of 1929*, 50.

STARTING LINE

102 "Today the eyes": "Feminine Air Racers Ready for Start," *Santa Monica (CA) Outlook*, August 18, 1929.

102 "Pick the Winner of the Women's Air Derby," *Santa Monica (CA) Outlook*, August 18, 1929.

103 "This race is going to show" and "It's going to take plenty": "Women Pilots to Hop Today at Shot Here," *Cleveland Plain Dealer*, August 18, 1929.

103 Bobbi Trout's race prep and lucky charm: "Women Fliers in Cleveland Derby All Have Mascots," *Green Bay (WI) Press-Gazette*, August 21, 1929.

104 "A third the breaks": Thaden, "The Women's Air Derby," *Aero Digest*, October 1929, 299.

104 "I'll wear a dress": "Women Pilots to Hop Today at Shot Here," *Cleveland Plain Dealer*, August 8, 1929.

104 "Flying fast will be hard work": "Women Flyers Speed to City," *Cleveland Plain Dealer*, August 19, 1929.

104 Scene at Clover Field: Jessen, *The Powder Puff Derby of 1929*, 54–66; "Officials Pleased at Fine Get-Away": *Santa Monica (CA) Outlook*, August 19, 1929; amazing film clips of racers and planes are included in Taylor, *Breaking Through the Clouds*.

104 "It was a madhouse" and "Don't worry": Thaden, *High, Wide, and Frightened*, 46.

105 "Well, Marvel" and "Thanks, Pancho": film clip included in Taylor, *Breaking Through the Clouds*.

105 "I don't care what you guys write": Kessler, *The Happy Bottom Riding Club*, 71.

105 "Well, it looks like a powder puff derby": Taylor, *Breaking Through the Clouds*.

105 "Ladybirds" and other nicknames: Jessen, *The Powder Puff Derby of 1929*, 59; these nicknames come up over and over in articles throughout the nine days of the race.

105 "We are still trying": Earhart, *The Fun of It*, 152.

105–106 Louise Thaden provides many great details, including the hot dog and her pre-race jitters: Thaden, *So They Flew*, an unpublished memoir of her Derby experience, available in the Louise McPhetridge Thaden Collection at the Smithsonian National Air and Space Museum Archives, Box 4, Folder 3.

106 Pancho feeling confident: Taylor, *Breaking Through the Clouds*.

106 "I would be far outclassed": Nichols, *Wings for Life*, 90.

106 O'Donnell's good-bye, including "Win the race or bust" and her reply: Doyle, *Second to None*, 84; Taylor, *Breaking Through the Clouds*.

106 "Don't hug me so tight": "Women Fliers in Cleveland Derby All Have Mascots," *Green Bay (WI) Press-Gazette*, August 21, 1929.

108 "Goodbye and good luck": Tordoff, *Mercy Pilot*, 101.

108 "I will now give you your final instructions": Taylor, *Breaking Through the Clouds*.

108 "You will receive ten drops": Thaden, *High, Wide, and Frightened*, 47.

108 "They're off!" and other commentary by Clover Field announcer: Taylor, *Breaking Through the Clouds*.

109 "That wife of yours had better": Corn, "Making Flying 'Thinkable': Women Pilots and the Selling of Aviation, 1927–1940," *American Quarterly*, Autumn 1979, 562.

110 "I won't say I was petrified": "Race Is Greatest Thrill of Life, Ruth Elder Says," *Wichita Eagle*, August 19, 1929.

110–111 Day One details: Jessen, *The Powder Puff Derby of 1929*, 69–70; "Wichita Planes Are Showing Tail Skids to Others in Derby," *Wichita Eagle*, August 19, 1929; "Throngs Seek Advantage to Greet Fliers," *San Bernardino Sun*, August 19, 1929.

SAN BERNARDINO

113 Omlie's life-changing moment: Sherman, *Walking on Air*, 5–6.

113 "Don't put it in the papers": Sherman, *Walking on Air*, 17.

115, 117 Day One details and results: "Throngs Seek Advantage to Greet Fliers," *San Bernardino Sun*, August 19, 1929; "Pilots and Time on First Lap," *Wichita Beacon*, August 19, 1929; Jessen, *The Powder Puff Derby of 1929*, 72–75.

117 "It's some feeling": "Throngs Seek Advantage to Greet Fliers," *San Bernardino Sun*, August 19, 1929.

118 "There is plenty of space": "Race Is Greatest Thrill of Life, Ruth Elder Says," *Wichita Eagle*, August 19, 1929.

118 "She could have made it": "Throngs Seek Advantage to Greet Fliers," *San Bernardino Sun*, August 19, 1929.

118–119 Pancho, who suspected sabotage, recalls Marvel's concerns: Tate, *The Lady Who Tamed Pegasus*, 46.

119 San Bernardino banquet: "Contestants Are Guests of Exchange Club," *San Bernardino Sun*, August 19, 1929; Jessen, *The Powder Puff Derby of 1929*, 81.

119 Marvel's friend recalls her feeling ill on first evening of race: "No Traces of Interference Found at Quiz," *San Bernardino Sun*, August 22, 1929.

119–120 Pancho and the other pilots demand route change: "Women Pilots Force Change of Routing in National Derby," *Calexico (CA) Chronicle*, August 19, 1929; "Girl Air Racers Revolt: Threaten Strike," *San Bernardino Sun*, August 20, 1929; Jessen, *The Powder Puff Derby of 1929*, 81–82.

120 "Wisps of gray fog": Thaden, *High, Wide, and Frightened*, 48.

121 Problems at San Bernardino: Jessen, *The Powder Puff Derby of 1929*, 93–94; "Girl Flier's Death Starts Quiz into Air Derby Sabotage Charge," *San Bernardino Sun*, August 21, 1929; Thaden, *So They Flew*, 7.

121 "I'm going to get every last bit": Jessen, *The Powder Puff Derby of 1929*, 95.

121 "Oh, bugs!": Veca, *Just Plane Crazy*, 116.

122 "Women Fliers Begin Air Derby": *New York Times*, August 19, 1929; "Young Pilots Hop Off in First Women's Air Derby": *Burlington (VT) Free Press*, August 19, 1929; "Fair Fliers Speed Across Country in Air Derby": (Coshocton, OH) *Tribune*, August 19, 1929.

122 Day Two begins: Jessen, *The Powder Puff Derby of 1929*, 95–96; Thaden, *So They Flew*, 8.

TROUBLES BEGIN

124 Ruth Elder's Day Two troubles: "Women Flyers Reach City," *Arizona Republican*, August 20, 1929; Jessen, *The Powder Puff Derby of 1929*, 98–100.

125 "The fact that I was over a field": "Suggest Delaying Race," *New York Times*, August 21, 1929.

125 "rubber, fiber, and many other impurities": Jessen, *The Powder Puff Derby*, 112.

126 "But I never saw gasoline": "Women Fliers Have Little to Say About Sabotage Question," *Wichita Eagle*, August 24, 1929.

126 "Must be dirt in the carburetor": Taylor includes excerpts from an audio recording of Bobbi Trout in her film, *Breaking Through the Clouds*; more on Trout's forced landing: Veca, *Just Plane Crazy*, 120–121.

127–128 Earhart's rough landing in Yuma: "Amelia Breaks Propeller at Yuma Airport," *El Paso Evening Post*, August 19, 1929; "Amelia Earhart Noses Over Plane at Yuma," *Wichita Eagle*, August 20, 1929.

128 "If you all will allow me": Thaden, *So They Flew*, 9.

128 "Have you ever stood": Thaden, *High, Wide, and Frightened*, 48.

128 "I really thought": "We Really Were Trailblazers," *Arizona Republic*, August 6, 1972.

128 "The first plane will leave": Thaden, *High, Wide, and Frightened*, 48; Thaden describes the rough flight to Phoenix: Thaden, *High, Wide, and Frightened*, 48–50; Thaden, *So They Flew*, 10–11.

131 Pilots arrive in Phoenix, including quotes from Elder and Miller: "Women Flyers Reach City," *Arizona Republican*, August 20, 1929.

132 "Going to have to watch": Thaden, *So They Flew*, 13.

132 "Now what the hell": Thaden, *So They Flew*, 12.

132 Phoenix banquet: "Famous Women Flyers Are Honor Guests at Exchange Club Banquet," *Arizona Republican*, August 19, 1929; "Derby Flyers Prove Feminine Aviation Is 13-Sided Affair," *Arizona Republican*, August 19, 1929.

132 "Marvel Crosson is down" and Marvel rumors: Thaden, *High, Wide, and Frightened*,

50; "One Flier Missing, Three Ships Down on Second Lap of Air Race," *San Bernardino Sun*, August 20, 1929.

133 Earhart and Miller talk in their room: Spicer, *The Flying Adventures of Jessie Keith "Chubbie" Miller*, 107.

134 "We're all as tired": "Squabble over Fields Robs Women Derbyists of Rest," *Wichita Eagle*, August 20, 1929.

MARVEL

135 "Discouraged searching parties": "Ranchers See Plane Similar to Crosson's Fall in Trees," *Albuquerque Journal*, August 20, 1929; "Believe Flier Is Killed," (Yuma, AZ) *Morning Sun*, August 20, 1929.

135 "filled with foreboding": "Girl Racer Killed," Associated Press article from Phoenix, *Kansas City Star*, August 20, 1929.

136 "I am convinced": "Sabotage Charged by Flyer," *Arizona Republican*, August 21, 1929.

136 "The wires show evidence": "Believe Flyer Is Killed," (Yuma, AZ) *Morning Sun*, August 20, 1929.

136 "Of course, tampering with the planes": "Girl Flier's Death Starts Quiz into Air Derby Sabotage Charge," *San Bernardino Sun*, August 21, 1929.

136 "told a very suspicious story" and Trout update: "Crash Probes Launched," (Yuma, AZ) *Morning Sun*, August 20, 1929; Veca, *Just Plane Crazy*, 124–125.

137 "I was told by several people": Taylor, *Breaking Through the Clouds*.

137 "I am afraid I broke": Earhart, *The Fun of It*, 93.

137–138 Pancho's Mexico detour: Jessen, *The Powder Puff Derby of 1929*, 108; Thaden, *High, Wide, and Frightened*, 50.

137–138 Pilots' flight to Douglas: Jessen, *The Powder Puff Derby of 1929*, 122–124; "Aviatrix Loses Time in Salute at Casa Grande," *Arizona Republican*, August 21, 1929; Thaden, *High, Wide, and Frightened*, 50.

139 Marvel found: "Miss Crosson Dies in Crash Near Wellton," *Arizona Republican*, August 21, 1929; "Official Investigators Are Here to View Death Plane," (Yuma, AZ) *Morning Sun*, August 21, 1929; "Woman Flyer Dies, Tangles in Parachute," *Dallas Morning News*, August 21, 1929; "Crosson Death Makes Women Flyers Weep," *El Paso Evening Post*, August 20, 1929.

140 "Women can do men's work": Crosson, "How I Learned to Fly," *The Country Gentleman*, September 1929, 100.

140 "Mrs. Thaden and Mrs. O'Donnell": "Air Inquiry Launched," *Los Angeles Times*, August 21, 1929.

140–141 Crash investigation and theories: "Girl Flier's Death Starts Quiz into Air Derby Sabotage Charge," *San Bernardino Sun*, August 21, 1929; "Sabotage Charged by Flyer," *Arizona Republican*, August 21, 1929; "Wichita Woman Flier Leads Derby," *Wichita Eagle*, August 20, 1929; Tordoff, *Mercy Pilot*, 100; Jessen, *The Powder Puff Derby of 1929*, 129; Thaden, *High, Wide, and Frightened*, 51.

141 "Words cannot express": "Marvel Crosson's Folks Will Get Cup if Wichita Flier Wins Derby," *Wichita Eagle*, August 21, 1929.

143 Thaden and Earhart talk in the Douglas Hotel: Jessen, *The Powder Puff Derby of 1929*, 133–134.

CRITICS ATTACK

144 "Women Have Conclusively Proven They Cannot Fly" and "Women's Derby Should Be Terminated": Thaden, *High, Wide, and Frightened*, 51; "Airplane Races Too Hazardous an Adventure for Women Pilots" and "Air racing for women should be discouraged": *New York American*, August 21, 1929.

144 "Such races are all right": "Council Raps Women's Race," *El Paso Evening Post*, August 20, 1929.

144 "youth and charm like hers": *Knoxville Journal* excerpt found in "The Women's Air Derby," *The Literary Digest*, September 7, 1929, 9.

145 "The derby will go on": "Fail to See Sabotage in Plane Wreck," (Yuma, AZ) *Morning Sun*, August 22, 1929.

145 "Fly with all precaution": "No Traces of Interference Found at Quiz," *San Bernardino Sun*, August 22, 1929.

146 "The only thing I worried about": "Mrs. Thaden Tells Own Story of How She Won Derby Race," *Pittsburgh Post-Gazette*, August 27, 1929.

146 "It is now all the more necessary": Kessler, *The Happy Bottom Riding Club*, 72.

146 "Mexico or Bust": Taylor, *Breaking Through the Clouds*: Lou D'Elia of the Pancho Barnes Trust Estate tells this story in bonus interviews included on the DVD.

146 Day Four flights: "Derby Flyers Finish Douglas Lap," *Arizona Republican*, August 21, 1929; "Fliers to Spend Night Here," *El Paso Herald*, August 21, 1929; "Women Flyers Spend Night in Paso," *El Paso Evening Post*, August 21, 1929; "Sandstorm Halts Women's Air Race," *Wichita Eagle*, August 22, 1929; Jessen, *The Powder Puff Derby of 1929*, 137–138.

147 "Gladys O'Donnell didn't bother": "Fliers to Spend Night Here," *El Paso Herald*, August 21, 1929.

147 "that a powerful gambling ring": "Official Investigators Are Here to View Death Plane" (Yuma, AZ) *Morning Sun*, August 21, 1929.

147 Null's conclusions: "Heat Is Blamed," *Arizona Republican*, August 22, 1929; "Fail to See Sabotage in Plane Wreck," (Yuma, AZ) *Morning Sun*, August 22, 1929; Pete Hill disagrees: Jessen, *The Powder Puff Derby of 1929*, 153, 210.

148 Coroner's inquest: "Official Investigators Are Here to View Death Plane," (Yuma, AZ) *Morning Sun*, August 21, 1929.

148 "If we agree to go ahead" and "It is much better": "Women Flyers Spend Night in Paso," *El Paso Evening Post*, August 21, 1929.

149 "Most of the flyers refused": "Famous Women Flyers Eat Dinner at Juarez Cafe," *El Paso Evening Post*, August 22, 1929; Pancho drinks beer: Jessen, *The Powder Puff Derby of 1929*, 149.

149 "The strain of competition": "Strain Is Telling," *Wichita Eagle*, August 22, 1929.

149 "We admire, after a fashion": "Women Fliers Out of Place," *Muncie (IN) Morning Star*, August 22, 1929.

149–150 "Women have been dependent": Jessen, *The Powder Puff Derby of 1929*, 128.

150 "We women pilots were blazing": Thaden, *High, Wide, and Frightened*, 51.

150 Day Five begins: "Amelia Earhart Takes Derby Lead," *El Paso Evening Post*, August 22, 1929; "Women Fliers Leave El Paso," *El Paso Herald*, August 22, 1929.

ACROSS TEXAS

152 Standings in El Paso: "Women Flyers Spend Night in Paso," *El Paso Evening Post*, August 21, 1929.

153 "You can't get mad" and "I won't tell": "Mrs. Barnes Takes Bad Luck with Smile," *El Paso Herald*, August 22, 1929.

153, 155–156 Blanche Noyes's fire: "Fire in Derby Plane Halts Woman Flier," *New York Times*, August 23, 1929; "Earhart Taking Derby Lead," *Cleveland Plain Dealer*, August 23, 1929; "Mrs. Noyes Tells of Fire Fighting High Above Texas," *Cleveland Plain Dealer*, August 27, 1929; Thaden, *High, Wide, and Frightened*, 53–54; Jessen, *The Powder Puff Derby of 1929*, 150–152.

156–157 Pancho's crash in Pecos: "Louise Thaden Leads Derby to Pecos," *Pecos (TX) Enterprise and Gusher*, August 23, 1929; "Three Crash at Pecos Port," *El Paso Evening Post*,

August 22, 1929; Kessler, *The Happy Bottom Riding Club*, 73; Thaden, *High, Wide, and Frightened*, 53; Jessen, *The Powder Puff Derby of 1929*, 149–150; Taylor, *Breaking Through the Clouds*.

157 "It's going to crack up!" and Thaden recalls Noyes's landing in Pecos and their conversation: Thaden, *High, Wide, and Frightened*, 53–54.

157 "One of the big differences": Thaden, *High, Wide, and Frightened*, 54.

157–158 "It is doubtful whether Mr. Halliburton": "Hangar Yarns," *Wichita Beacon*, August 25, 1929.

158 "I figured to cut a few corners": Thaden, *So They Flew*, 20.

158 Midland standings: "Amelia Earhart Takes Derby Lead," *El Paso Evening Post*, August 22, 1929.

159–160 Chubbie Miller's snake story: Miller, "Our Flight to Australia," *Table Talk Magazine*, May 17, 1928, 24–26; Spicer, *The Flying Adventures of Jessie Keith "Chubbie" Miller*, 50–53.

160 Miller's twister experience: "Whirlwind Tosses Derby Race Plane" *Daily Oklahoman*, August 23, 1929; Spicer, *The Flying Adventures of Jessie Keith "Chubbie" Miller*, 111.

160 "We have not been able to find": "Sabotage Claim Unsupported by Investigations," *Albuquerque Journal*, August 23, 1929.

160 Racers in Abilene: "Crowds Greet Racers Here," *Abilene (TX) Morning News*, August 23, 1929; "Vera Walker Is Made Welcome by Her Dad," *Abilene (TX) Morning News*, August 23, 1929.

162 "There'll be no sabotage": "Racers Due Here Late Today," *Abilene (TX) Morning News*, August 22, 1929.

162 "At Fort Worth": Thaden, *High, Wide, and Frightened*, 52.

163 "The surging throng": "Derby Fliers Spend Night Here," *Fort Worth Star-Telegram*, August 23, 1929.

163 Thaden recalls the Fort Worth banquet, including song lyrics: Thaden, *So They Flew*, 24–25.

165 "That's all we've been fed": Doyle, *Second to None*, 100.

165 "Do you wonder we were tired": Thaden, "The Women's Air Derby," *Aero Digest*, October 1929, 62.

BACK TO WICHITA

166 Pancho's reaction to being out of the race: Tate, *The Lady Who Tamed Pegasus*, 47; Schultz, *Pancho*, 74; "Florence Barnes to Leave Wichita Today," *Wichita Eagle*, August 25, 1929.

167 "We don't want those girls": "Women Fliers Halted by Storms," *Fort Worth Star-Telegram*, August 22, 1929.

167 "For a pilot to be sick": "Influenza Forces Mrs. Perry from Race," *Fort Worth Star-Telegram*, August 24, 1929; "Had Typhoid Fever," *Dallas Morning News*, August 25, 1929.

168 "I was flying serenely along": Thaden, *High, Wide, and Frightened*, 53; "Fliers Winging Way to Wichita," *Wichita Beacon*, August 23, 1929; Jessen, *The Powder Puff Derby of 1929*, 109–110.

168 "It didn't make any difference": "Ladybirds in Kansas," *Los Angeles Times*, August 24, 1929.

170 Tulsa updates: "Mrs. Thaden Leads Race to Wichita," *Fort Worth Star-Telegram*, August 24, 1929; "Women Fliers Land at Tulsa," *Miami (OK) Daily News-Record*, August 23, 1929.

170 "Sure, I'm gonna catch up": "Bobbi Trout, Last of Women Fliers to Reach El Paso, Is Philosophical," *El Paso Herald*, August 24, 1929.

170–171 Halliburton quotes: "Air Line Head Asks Race Be Discontinued," *El Paso Evening Post*, August 23, 1929; "Thaden Is Retaining Air Lead," *Wichita Eagle*, August 24, 1929.

171 "Don't be foolish": Doyle, *Second to None*, 100.

171 "I never heard of anything" and "Who is this man Halliburton": "Girls Peeved," *Pittsburgh Press*, August 25, 1929.

172 Thaden describes her nerve-racking trip to Wichita: Thaden, *High, Wide, and Frightened*, 55; Thaden, *So They Flew*, 28; "Back Home and Happy," *Wichita Eagle*, August 24, 1929.

172 "Swell going, fella" and "Hi, Pal!": Thaden, *High, Wide, and Frightened*, 55.

173 Copeland's remarks in Wichita: "Louise von Thaden First to Wichita," *Wichita Eagle*, August 24, 1929; Jessen, *The Powder Puff Derby of 1929*, 129.

174 Marvel Crosson's funeral: "Aviatrix Paid Last Tributes," *Los Angeles Times*, August 24, 1929; "Throng Attends Simple Funeral for Girl Flyer," *San Diego Union*, August 24, 1929.

174 "Any one of thousands" and "And now to cap it all": "Women Fliers Have Little to Say About Sabotage Question," *Wichita Eagle*, August 24, 1929.

175 "I was glad" and "I am almost ashamed": "Wichita in Mighty Gesture of Welcome to Women Aviators," *Wichita Eagle*, August 24, 1929.

176 "Well, I feel now more": "Back Home and Happy," *Wichita Eagle*, August 24, 1929.

THE GRIND

177 Ruth Elder engagement rumors: "Ruth Elder to Wed Camp, Jr.," *Wichita Eagle*, August 25, 1929; "Ruth Elder Admits She Will Wed Camp," *St. Louis Post-Dispatch*, August 25, 1929.

177–178 O'Donnell engagement rumors and her response: Doyle, *Second to None*, 98.

178 "I'm pushing her" and "Aye, your blithering deserts" and "After the desert": "Their Noses First," *Kansas City Star*, August 24, 1929.

179 Thaden's close call at East St. Louis: Thaden, *So They Flew*, 35–36.

180 "Can I catch them": "Bobbie Trout Hopes to Catch up With Derby Fliers Today," *Wichita Eagle*, August 25, 1929.

181 "Will Miss Elder do any more flying": "Walter Camp Wins Ruth, But Won't Be 'Mr. Elder'," *New York Daily News*, August 25, 1929.

181 Day Seven standings: "Racers into St. Louis," *Kansas City Star*, August 25, 1929.

181 "Well, here we are": "Nerves Growing Taut," *Wichita Eagle*, August 25, 1929.

182–183 Thaden describes the early-morning scene on Day Eight: Thaden, *High, Wide, and Frightened*, 56; Jessen, *The Powder Puff Derby of 1929*, 187.

183 Terre Haute stop: Jessen, *The Powder Puff Derby of 1929*, 188; Thaden, *So They Flew*, 41–42.

184 "Miss Earhart had made": Lovell, *The Sound of Wings*, 135.

184 Putnam's forced landing in Ohio and "If you'd sighted": Putnam, *Wide Margins*, 286–287.

185 Edith Foltz mishap and Trout down again: "Ladybirds Ending Derby Flight," *Xenia (OH) Evening Gazette*, August 26, 1929; Veca, *Just Plane Crazy*, 126.

185 "I have all the confidence": "Louise Liked Toy Engines Better Than Dolls, Says Dad," *Wichita Eagle*, August 26, 1929.

186 "chief interest here centers": "Cleveland Watches for Women Fliers," *New York Times*, August 24, 1929.

186 "See that Herb!" and Thaden's reception in Columbus: Thaden, *High, Wide, and Frightened*, 56; Louise Thaden's daughter, Pat Thaden Webb, tells the story in bonus material included with the DVD of Taylor, *Breaking Through the Clouds*.

187 "You can have anything": "Mrs. Thaden Seen as Derby Winner," *Cleveland Plain Dealer*, August 26, 1929.

187 "Breast of Chicken on Toast": an original menu from the Columbus banquet can be found in the Louise McPhetridge Thaden Collection, the Smithsonian National Air and Space Museum Archives, Box 1, Folder 21.

187 "Somehow this final night": "Regret Derby End," *Wichita Eagle*, August 26, 1929.

FINISH LINE

190–192 Ruth Nichols recalls her test flight and crash in Nichols, *Wings for Life*, 90–92.

192 "How's she running, Johnnie?": Thaden, *So They Flew*, 54.

192 "Now don't get excited" and Herb's other nervous chatter: Thaden, *High, Wide, and Frightened*, 57.

193 Louise Thaden describes her takeoff for Cleveland: Thaden, *High, Wide, and Frightened*, 58.

193 Scene at the Cleveland Airport: "Forget Planes as Lindberghs Land," *Cleveland Plain Dealer*, August 27, 1929.

193 "I've been flying airplanes": "Florence Barnes to Leave Wichita Today," *Wichita Eagle*, August 25, 1929.

193 "Is aviation a woman's game": "Mrs. Thaden Is Derby Victor," *Cleveland Plain Dealer*, August 27, 1929.

193 "Halfway there" and Thaden's flight to Cleveland: Thaden, *High, Wide, and Frightened*, 58; Thaden, *So They Flew*, 56–58; "Mrs. Thaden Tells Own Story of How She Won Derby Race," *Pittsburgh Post-Gazette*, August 27, 1929.

194 "Mrs. Thaden, how does it feel" and other details of her moment of victory: Thaden, *High, Wide, and Frightened*, 58–59; Thaden, *So They Flew*, 58; "Mrs. Thaden Is Derby Victor," *Cleveland Plain Dealer*, August 27, 1929; "Mrs. Thaden Winner," *Los Angeles Times*, August 27, 1929; "Mrs. Thaden Gives Plane Credit for Derby Victory," *Pittsburgh Post-Gazette*, August 27, 1929; great footage of this moment can be seen in Taylor, *Breaking Through the Clouds*.

196 "Thrilled?": Doyle, *Second to None*, 103.

197 "But at that moment": Smith, *Aviatrix*, 133.

197 "Don't light that here!": "Mrs. Thaden Is Derby Victor," *Cleveland Plain Dealer*, August 27, 1929.

198 "A wonderful, wonderful experience": "Mrs. Noyes Tells of Fire Fighting High Above Texas," *Cleveland Plain Dealer*, August 27, 1929.

198 "I saw this nice field": "New Zealand Lady Derby Flyer Lands on Farm Near Xenia," *Xenia (OH) Evening Gazette*, August 26, 1929.

198 Ruth Elder's Akron detour: Taylor, *Breaking Through the Clouds*; "Mrs. Thaden Is Derby Victor," *Cleveland Plain Dealer*, August 27, 1929.

199 Women's Air Derby final standings: "Mrs. Thaden Is Derby Victor," *Cleveland Plain Dealer*, August 27, 1929.

199 "I'm frank to admit" and highest percentage of finishers: "Women Flyers Real Sports," *Cleveland Plain Dealer*, August 26, 1929.

200 "If ever there was a question": Matowitz, *Images of America*, 11.

200 Thaden's telegram: Taylor, *Breaking Through the Clouds*.

200 "I was rather confident": "R. F. McPhetridge Wichita's Happiest Man Monday Night," *Wichita Eagle*, August 28, 1929.

200 "How was the race?" and this Cleveland Airport scene: "Mrs. Thaden Is Derby Victor," *Cleveland Plain Dealer*, August 27, 1929.

200–201 Banquet details: Doyle, *Second to None*, 106; Taylor, *Breaking Through the Clouds*; Veca, *Just Plane Crazy*, 127; Kessler, *The Happy Bottom Riding Club*, 75.

201 "Much later I heard": Smith, *Aviatrix*, 134.

202 "I was sure she'd win": Herb Thaden's quote appears in the caption of the photo of him smiling at the finish line in the *Pittsburgh Press*, August 27, 1929.

202 "I think we have proved": Thaden, "The Women's Air Derby," *Aero Digest*, October 1929, 299.

202 Thaden gives cup to Crosson family: "Dedicate Cup to Memory of Sister Flier," *Wichita Eagle*, August 27, 1929; Thaden, "The Women's Air Derby," *Aero Digest*, October 1929, 62.

RACING THE ATLANTIC, THE SEQUEL

203 "It is almost impossible": "Dedicate Cup to Memory of Sister Flier," *Wichita Eagle*, August 27, 1929.

203 Founding of Ninety-Nines: Jessen, *The Powder Puff Derby of 1929*, 211; Brooks-Pazmany, *United States Women in Aviation, 1919–1929*, 51–52; more on the Ninety-Nines' history and current programs at ninety-nines.org. The organization also maintains the 99s Museum of Women Pilots in Oklahoma City, which houses a huge collection of displays and archives.

205 Thaden recalls wrestling Earhart: Thaden, "Amelia," *Air Facts*, July 1970, 53.

205 "I think we would be willing": Thaden, "The Women's Air Derby," *Aero Digest*, October 1929, 299.

206 Trout and Smith's endurance flights: "Girl Endurance Flyers Run Short on Fuel Again," *Los Angeles Times*, November 29, 1929; Veca, *Just Plane Crazy*, 136–146; Smith, *Aviatrix*, 183, 194.

207 Pancho's speed record: "Aviatrix Sets Speed Record," *Los Angeles Times*, August 5, 1930.

207 "Yes, Ruth is bound": Nichols, *Wings for Life*, 140.

207–208 Nichols describes her crash in Canada and the bad news from the doctor: Nichols, *Wings for Life*, 152–163.

209 "You know, Ruth": Nichols, *Wings for Life*, 209.

209 Earhart describes her Atlantic preparations: Earhart, *The Fun of It*, 209–213.

209–210 Earhart's solo Atlantic flight: Earhart, *The Fun of It*, 213–218; Putnam, *Soaring Wings*, 98–110; Lovell, *The Sound of Wings*, 179–182; "Amelia Earhart, Flying Solo, Spans Atlantic," *New York Daily News*, May 22, 1932; "Mrs. Putnam Flies Atlantic to Ireland," *New York Times*, May 22, 1932.

EPILOGUE: THE RACE GOES ON

212 "I felt pretty low" and Nichols's telegram to Earhart: Nichols, *Wings for Life*, 210; "Rivals Praise Amelia's Feat," *Pittsburgh Press*, May 22, 1932.

212 For a good summary of Nichols's flight records, see the Ruth Nichols page at the Smithsonian National Air and Space Museum's "Women in Aviation and Space History" website.

213 "Family and friends have urged": Nichols, *Wings for Life*, 18.

213 Gladys O'Donnell wins 1930 race: Doyle, *Second to None*, 136–142.

213–214 Blanche Noyes wrap-up: Oakes, *United States Women in Aviation, 1930–1939*, 14.

214 Claire Fahy and Neva Paris crashes: "Claire Fahy Badly Hurt in Crack-Up," *Los Angeles Times*, December 16, 1930; "Mrs. Claire Fahy Dies of Injuries," *Boston Globe*, December 19, 1930; "Mrs. Neva Paris Crashes Near Georgia Town," *Tampa Times*, January 9, 1930.

214 Summaries of the post-Women's Air Derby flying adventures of all the pilots, including May Haizlip, Opal Kunz, Margaret Perry, and Vera Dawn Walker, can be found in the epilogue of Jessen, *The Powder Puff Derby of 1929*.

214 Omlie's political campaigning and meeting with FDR: Sherman, *Walking on Air*, 75–76; "Aviator Omlie Soared to Success," *Des Moines Register*, July 27, 2008.

214–215 Thea Rasche and Nazis: "Thea Rasche Insists She Wouldn't Fly for Nazis," *Chicago Tribune*, July 26, 1945; "Germans Clear Flying Fraulein," *Los Angeles Times*, May 24, 1947.

215–216 Chubbie Miller's postrace life: Spicer, *The Flying Adventures of Jessie Keith "Chubbie" Miller*, 154–205; "Search to Tell Story of Dashing Aviation," (Queensland, Australia) *Courier-Mail*, March 16, 2013; "First Woman to Fly from England to Australia, Jessie Miller," (Queensland, Australia) *Courier-Mail*, March 22, 2017.

216–217 Elinor Smith wrap-up: Smith, *Aviatrix*, 288–289; "Elinor Smith, One of the Youngest Pioneers of Aviation, Is Dead at 98," *New York Times*, March 27, 2010; "Saying Goodbye to One of America's Earliest Female Aviation Pioneers: Elinor Smith Sullivan," Smithsonian.com, March 30, 2010.

217 Bobbi Trout's adventures: Veca, *Just Plane Crazy*, 163–184; the "Bobbi Evelyn Trout" page at ninety-nines.org has a good summary of her flying life; "Pioneer of Flight Lends Expo an Air of History," *Los Angeles Times*, July 11, 1999.

217 "I hated like the deuce": Veca, *Just Plane Crazy*, 181.

217 "When women did something": "Evelyn 'Bobbi' Trout, 97; Record-Setting Aviatrix of the 1920s," *Los Angeles Times*, January 30, 2003.

217 "Every woman before me": "A Soaring Tribute to a Pioneer," *Los Angeles Times*, February 24, 2003.

218 "I believe in the independence": "Ruth Elder Hopes to Make Another Ocean Flight," *Minneapolis Star Tribune*, June 22, 1928.

218 "They were more terrifying" and "There is nothing like the whir": "Ruth Elder, Saved Because Boat Was Delayed, Is Feted," *Minneapolis Star Tribune*, June 20, 1928.

218 Elder recalls flying memories: "Ruth Elder: From Beauty Contestant to Heroine," *Anniston (AL) Star*, July 4, 1976; more postrace details: "Flamboyant Aviator Ruth Elder Dies at 74," *Los Angeles Times*, October 11, 1977.

218–219 Pancho's postrace life: Kessler, *The Happy Bottom Riding Club*, chapters 8–21; Schultz, *Pancho*, chapters 11–27; Wolfe, *The Right Stuff*, 40–41; the story is also well told, with photos and footage of Pancho throughout her life, in the documentary *The Legend of Pancho Barnes and the Happy Bottom Riding Club* by Nick Spark and Amanda Pope.

219 "Marvel Crosson's Kid Brother Flies On": headline and Elizabeth Crosson quotes are from the (St. Petersburg) *Evening Independent*, December 6, 1929; Joe Crosson's life is the subject of *Mercy Pilot* by Dick Tordoff.

220 "*Something* happened": from an interview with Bobbi Trout by Helen Whittaker, in Women's Air Derby folder in archives of the Ninety-Nines' museum.

220 "There was a lot of dirty work": Schultz, *Pancho*, 75; "There was a lot of sabotage": "Pancho's Kind Fading—She's Pure Individual," *Long Beach Independent Press-Telegram*, October 13, 1968.

221 "It's Louise Thaden!": Adams, *Heroines of the Sky*, 119.

221 1936 Bendix race details: Oakes, *United States Women in Aviation, 1930–1939*, 29–30; Thaden, *High, Wide, and Frightened*, 109–121; "Miss Thaden Wins Bendix Air Race," *Los Angeles Times*, September 5, 1936.

221 "We think you've won" and "This is no time for joking": Thaden, *High, Wide, and Frightened*, 119.

221 "Through the immediate years": Thaden, *High, Wide, and Frightened*, prologue.

223 Sally Ride and reaction: "Ride, Sally Ride," *New York Daily News*, June 19, 1983; "Cool, Versatile Astronaut: Sally Kristen Ride," *New York Times*, June 19, 1983; "American Woman Who Shattered Space Ceiling," *New York Times*, July 23, 2012.

223 Astronauts paying tribute to derby pilots: Jessen, *The Powder Puff Derby of 1929*, 201.

223, 225 Louise Thaden's daughter, Pat Thaden Webb, shared details of her childhood with me in September 2018; Louise Thaden recalls flying with her son in a T-33: Thaden, *High, Wide, and Frightened*, 161.

225–227 Muriel Earhart Morrissey dedicates chapters 17–20 of *Amelia, My Courageous Sister* to Earhart's around-the-world flight and disappearance; Lovell, *The Sound of Wings*, chapters 19–22; Burke, *Winged Legend*, chapters 15–20.

225 "I have a feeling": Putnam, *Soaring Wings*, 290.

226 "We must be on you" and "We are circling": Moolman, *Women Aloft*, 128; Adler, "Will the Search for Amelia Earhart Ever End?" *Smithsonian Magazine*, January 2015.

227 "I believe she went down": Snook, *I Taught Amelia to Fly*, 167.

227 "Amelia flew on across" and other pilots' opinions: Burke, *Winged Legend*, 235.

227-228 Louise Thaden describes her final meeting with Amelia Earhart: Thaden, *High, Wide, and Frightened*, 147–152; Thaden, "Amelia." *Air Facts*, July 1970, 52–55.

WORKS CITED

BOOKS, MAGAZINES, AND DOCUMENTARIES

Adams, Jean, and Margaret Kimball. *Heroines of the Sky*. New York: Doubleday, Doran & Company, 1942.

Adler, Jerry. "Will the Search for Amelia Earhart Ever End?" *Smithsonian Magazine*, January, 2015.

Allen, Frederick Lewis. *Only Yesterday: An Informal History of the 1920s*. New York: Harper & Row, 1931.

Backus, Jean L. *Letters from Amelia*. Boston: Beacon Press, 1982.

Bell, Elizabeth. *Sisters of the Wind: Voices of Early Women Aviators*. Pasadena, CA: Trilogy Books, 1994.

Brooks-Pazmany, Kathleen. *United States Women in Aviation, 1919–1929*. Washington, DC: Smithsonian Institution Press, 1991.

Brown, Margery. "What Men Flyers Think of Women Pilots." *Aeronautics*, March 1929, 62–64.

Buffington, Glenn. "We Call Her Bobbi Trout." *Vintage Airplane*, July 1981, 14–15.

Burke, John. *Winged Legend: The Story of Amelia Earhart*. New York: G. P. Putnam's Sons, 1970.

Butler, Susan. *East to the Dawn: The Life of Amelia Earhart*. New York: Da Capo Press, 2009.

Collins, Gail. *American Women: 400 Years of Dolls, Drudges, Helpmates, and Heroines*. New York: HarperCollins Publishers, 2003.

Copeland, Frank T. "The Women's Air Derby and Why." *Aeronautics*, May 1939, 386, 412.

Corn, Joseph J. "Making Flying 'Thinkable': Women Pilots and the Selling of Aviation, 1927–1940." *American Quarterly*, Vol. 31, No. 4 (Autumn 1979), 556–571.

Corn, Joseph J. *Winged Gospel: America's Romance with Aviation, 1900–1950*. New York: Oxford University Press, 1983.

Crosson, Marvel. "How I Learned to Fly." *The Country Gentleman*, September 1929, 26, 96, 98, 100.

Crosson, Marvel. Letters to Ms. Hagen, 1927–1928, in possession of Crosson family and used by permission.

Downie, Don. "Fabulous Pancho Barnes." *Flying*, March 1949, 36–37, 59–60.

Doyle, Lorraine O'Donnell. *Second to None: The Story of Lloyd & Gladys O'Donnell and the 1929 Women's Air Derby*. Rancho Santa Fe, CA: LSDS Publishing, 2001.

Dumenil, Lynn. *Modern Temper: American Culture and Society in the 1920s*. New York: Hill and Wang, 1995.

Earhart, Amelia. *20 Hrs. 40 Min: Our Flight in the Friendship*. New York: G.P. Putnam's Sons, 1928.

Earhart, Amelia. *The Fun of It*. New York: Brewer, Warren & Putman, 1932.

Earhart, Amelia. *Last Flight*. New York: Harcourt, Brace and Company, 1937.

Gould, Bruce. "Milady Takes the Air." *North American Review*, Vol. 228, No. 6 (December 1929), 691–697.

Gwynn-Jones, Terry. *The Air Racers: Aviation's Golden Era, 1909–1936*. London: Pelham Books, 1984.

Hamlen, Joseph. *Flight Fever*. New York: Doubleday & Company, 1971.

Jackson, Joe. *Atlantic Fever: Lindbergh, His Competitors, and the Race to Cross the Atlantic*. New York: Farrar, Straus and Giroux, 2012.

Jaros, Dean. *Heroes Without Legacy: American Airwomen, 1912–1944*. Boulder, CO: University Press of Colorado, 1993.

Jessen, Gene Nora. *The Powder Puff Derby of 1929: The True Story of the First Women's Cross-Country Air Race*. Naperville, IL: Sourcebooks, Inc., 2002.

Kessler, Lauren. *The Happy Bottom Riding Club: The Life and Times of Pancho Barnes*. New York: Random House, 2000.

Lebow, Eileen F. *Before Amelia: Women Pilots in the Early Days of Aviation*. Washington, DC: Potomac Books, 2002.

Lomax, Judy. *Women of the Air*. New York: Dodd, Mead & Company, 1987.

Lovell, Mary S. *The Sound of Wings: The Life of Amelia Earhart*. New York: St. Martin's Press, 1989.

Martinelli, Kara. *Beyond the Powder: The Legacy of the First Women's Cross-Country Air Race*. Hemlock Films, 2015.

Matowitz, Thomas. *Images of America: Cleveland's National Air Races*. Charleston, SC: Arcadia Publishing, 2005.

Mattison, M.F. "A Girl Flies to Fame," *Pacific Flyer*, April 1929, 5–7.

Miller, Jessie. "Our Flight to Australia," *Table Talk Magazine*, May 17, 1928, 24–26.

Mitchell, Barbara. "Pancho Barnes: A Legend in Our Lifetime." This four-part series of articles appeared in *Hi-Desert Spectator* in 1963: January–February, 7–9, 30–31; March, 5–11; April, 4–11; May–June, 15–22.

Mondor, Colleen. "The Short, Brilliant Career of Alaska's First Woman Pilot." *Anchorage Daily News*, June 19, 2016.

Moolman, Valerie. *Women Aloft*. Alexandria, VA: Time-Life Books, 1981.

Morrissey, Muriel Earhart, and Carol L. Osborne. *Amelia, My Courageous Sister*. Santa Clara, CA: Osborne Publisher, 1987.

Naughton, Thomas. "The Birdmen at Belmont Park." *American Heritage*, Vol. 7, No. 3, 1956.

Nichols, Ruth. *Wings for Life*. Philadelphia: J. B. Lippincott Company, 1957.

Oakes, Claudia M. *United States Women in Aviation, 1930–1939*. Washington, DC: Smithsonian Institution Press, 1991.

"Pancho Barnes: A Legend in Her Own Time." *Virginia Aviation*, October–December 1980, 6–7.

Pope, Amanda, and Nick Spark. *The Legend of Pancho Barnes and the Happy Bottom Riding Club*. Nick Spark Productions, 2009.

Powell, Herbert F. "The 1929 National Air Races Get Under Way." *Aviation Week*, August 31, 1929, 464–465.

Putnam, George Palmer. *Soaring Wings: A Biography of Amelia Earhart*. New York: Harcourt, Brace and Company, 1939.

Putnam, George Palmer. *Wide Margins: The Autobiography of a Publisher*. New York: Harcourt, Brace and Company, 1942.

Railey, Hilton Howell. *Touch'd with Madness*. New York: Carrick & Evans, 1938.

Schultz, Barbara Hunter. *Pancho: The Biography of Florence Lowe Barnes*. Lancaster, CA: Little Buttes Publishing Co., 1996.

Sherman, Janann. *Walking on Air: The Aerial Adventures of Phoebe Omlie*. Jackson, MS: University Press of Mississippi, 2011.

Smith, Elinor. *Aviatrix*. New York: Harcourt Brace Jovanovich, 1981.

Southern, Neta Snook. *I Taught Amelia to Fly*. New York: Vantage Press, 1974.

Spicer, Chrystopher J. *The Flying Adventures of Jessie Keith "Chubbie" Miller, The Southern Hemisphere's First International Aviatrix*. Jefferson, NC: McFarland & Company, 2017.

Sumner, Sandi. *Women Pilots of Alaska: 37 Interviews and Profiles*. Jefferson, NC: McFarland & Company, 2005.

Tate, Grover Ted. *The Lady Who Tamed Pegasus: The Story of Pancho Barnes*. Los Angeles: Maverick Publications, 1984.

Taylor, Heather, *Breaking Through the Clouds: The First Women's National Air Derby*, 2010.

Thaden, Bill, and Pat Thaden Webb. "Louise Thaden: Pioneer Aviator." *Vintage Airplane*, April 1989, 20–25, and May 1989, 17–19.

Thaden, Louise. "Amelia." *Air Facts*, July 1970, 52–55.

Thaden, Louise. "Breaking Records in the Clouds," *St. Louis Post-Dispatch*, June 11, 1930.

Thaden, Louise. *High, Wide, and Frightened*. Fayetteville, AK: University of Arkansas Press, 2004. First published in 1938.

Thaden, Louise. *So They Flew*, unpublished memoir of the 1929 Women's Air Derby, Smithsonian Louise McPhetridge Thaden Collection, Box 4, Folder 3.

Thaden, Louise McPhetridge. "The Women's Air Derby." *Aero Digest*, October 1929, 62, 299.

"The American Girl." *Aero Digest*, November 1927, 515, 612.

"The American Super-Girl and Her Critics." *The Literary Digest*, October 29, 1927, 52–55.

"The Women's Air Derby," *The Literary Digest*, September 7, 1929, 9.

Tordoff, Dick. *Mercy Pilot: The Joe Crosson Story*. Kenmore, WA: Epicenter Press, 2002.

Veca, Donna, and Skip Mazzio. *Just Plane Crazy: Biography of Bobbi Trout*. Santa Clara, CA: Osborne Publishing, 1987.

Walker, Mike. *Powder Puff Derby: Petticoat Pilots and Flying Flappers*. Hoboken, NJ: Wiley, 2003.

Wischnia, Bob. "We Really Were Trailblazers." *Arizona Republic Magazine*, August 6, 1972, 56–62.

Wolfe, Tom. *The Right Stuff*. New York: Farrar, Straus and Giroux, 1979.

NEWSPAPERS

*Abilene (TX) Morning News**

Akron Beacon Journal

Albuquerque Journal

Anchorage Daily News

Anniston (AL) Star

*Arizona Republican** (renamed *Arizona Republic* in 1930)

Benton County (AK) Herald

Boston Globe

Brooklyn Daily Eagle

Burlington (VT) Free Press

Calexico (CA) Chronicle

Chicago Tribune

*Cincinnati Enquirer**

*Cleveland Herald Tribune**

*Cleveland Plain Dealer**

Coshocton (OH) *Tribune*

Courier-Mail (Queensland, Australia)

Daily Oklahoman

Dallas Morning News

Des Moines Register

Detroit Free Press

*El Paso Evening Post**

*El Paso Herald**

Fairbanks Daily News-Minor

Fort Lauderdale (FL) News

*Fort Worth Star-Telegram**

Green Bay (WI) Press Gazette

*Kansas City Star**

Knoxville (TN) Journal

London Daily News

Long Beach Independent Press-Telegram

Los Angeles Times

Manitowoc (WI) Herald Times

Miami (OK) Daily News-Record

Minneapolis Star Tribune

Muncie (IN) Morning Star

New York American

New York Daily News

New York Times

Northwest Arkansas Times

Oakland Tribune

Pecos (TX) Enterprise and Gusher*

Pittsburgh Press

Pittsburgh Post-Gazette

Poughkeepsie (NY) Eagle-News

Riverside (CA) Daily Press

Sacramento Union

San Bernardino Sun*

San Diego Evening Tribune

San Diego Union

San Francisco Call

San Francisco Chronicle

Santa Ana Register

Santa Maria (CA) Times

Santa Monica (CA) Outlook*

St. Louis Post-Dispatch

(St. Petersburg) *Evening Independent*

Tampa Times

Tulsa Daily World*

Warsaw (IN) Daily Times

Wichita Beacon*

Wichita Eagle*

Xenia (OH) Evening Gazette

(Yuma, AZ) *Morning Sun**

ACKNOWLEDGMENTS

This book began, though I didn't realize it at the time, in early 2017, when my good friend David Sewell McCann invited me to be a guest on his popular children's podcast, *Sparkle Stories*. David told the story of Blanche Noyes giving John D. Rockefeller his first and only plane ride, mentioning in passing that Noyes had been part of a groundbreaking race called the Women's Air Derby of 1929. I'd never heard of it. Then, a few weeks later, I checked into a hotel and turned on the TV as background noise while I unpacked, and I heard people talking about the Women's Air Derby of 1929. I stopped unpacking and watched the second half of Heather Taylor's excellent documentary on the race, *Breaking Through the Clouds*. I was hooked. So, first of all, thanks to David for introducing me to the story. And thanks to Heather, both for her film and for taking the time to share her unmatched knowledge of the pilots and the race.

There's not much on the Derby in book form, but one must-read is *The Powder Puff Derby of 1929* by Gene Nora Jessen. A pioneering pilot in her own right, Jessen is one of the women featured in Tanya Lee Stone's great book *Almost Astronauts*. She knew many of the Derby pilots and was kind enough to answer my questions about the racers.

From that point on, it was the usual nerdy detective work. Thank you to Dorothy Cochrane at the Smithsonian National Air and Space Museum for sharing background information and for putting me in touch with Pat Thaden Webb. And thanks to Pat for sharing memories and stories of her mother, Louise Thaden. Sue Marvel Fraser, Joe

Crosson's daughter, generously shared family photographs, including some priceless images of Marvel Crosson as a kid.

I quickly figured out that one of the few people who knows a lot about Marvel is an Alaska-based writer and pilot, Colleen Mondor. Thanks to Colleen for sharing her knowledge of Marvel and Joe, and to both her and her husband, Ward, also a pilot, for talking me through some of the technical details of early planes and all the things that can go wrong in the air. My friend Seth Rosan, a commercial pilot, also shared his incredible knowledge about the science of flight.

Thanks to librarians and helpful staff at The Ninety-Nines Museum of Women Pilots in Oklahoma City, the Smithsonian National Air and Space Museum archives, the Museum of Flying in Santa Monica, the New York Public Library, the Arizona Historical Society, and the Kansas Historical Society—and to libraries everywhere, especially the Saratoga Springs Public Library, my first stop for sources.

I am very grateful to the entire team at Roaring Brook Press and Macmillan for their continued support. Simon Boughton and Connie Hsu encouraged me to write this book, and Connie, super editor, worked with me every step of the way. Thank you to Jon Yaged, Jennifer Besser, Megan Abbate, Mekisha Telfer, Jill Freshney, Tracy Koontz, Morgan Dubin, Lucy Del Priore, Katie Halata, Cassie Gonzales, and Jen Keenan. My continued thanks also to Susan Cohen, Amy Berkower, and everyone at Writers House. And thanks to Bijou Karman for her amazing cover art and illustrations.

As always, my biggest thanks of all go to Rachel and our kids, Anna and David. Long before anything gets published, or even written, or even proposed to a publisher, they listen to all my ideas and stories and help me figure out which ones are good. Anna even sat with me for hours in the Air and Space Museum archives, pouring over Louise Thaden's letters and scrapbooks.

She declared them "pretty cool." There was no turning back—I *had* to tell this story.

PHOTO CREDITS

INDEX

Numbers in **bold** indicate pages with illustrations

B

Thaden, Louise McPhetridge "Lou," **120**, **180**; aggressive flying style of, 112; air derby entrance of, 79, **81**; air derby plane of, 79, 87, 92–94, 106, 134, **173**; altitude record-setting flight of, 66–70, **67**; Amelia's last visit with, 227–228; appearance of, 132, 147, **147**; Bendix speed race win by, 221, **222**; Bentonville flight with father, 88–89; bunking with Blanche during race, 134; Burke sleeping in plane of, 183, 189; carbon monoxide poisoning of, 93–94; carbon monoxide poisoning of Marvel, speculation about, 141; celebrity status and inspiration of, 223, 225; confidence of father in, 185, 200; continuing race after Marvel's death, pilots agreement about, 141, 143, 146, 150; crash and injury of, 64–66; damage to plane in St. Louis, 182–183; death of Marvel, reaction to, 140; derby start of, 109–110; early life of, 1, 5, **7**, 18; eighth leg flight of, 186; endurance record flights of, 73, 223; factors in winning race, 104, 176; fearlessness of pilots, belief about, 66; fifth leg flight of, 156, 158, 161, 162; final standings and overall time for, 199; first flight of, 18; first leg finish by, 115, 117; first-place finish by, 194–196, **195**, **197**, 199, 225; flying career of, 223, 225; flying lessons of, 41; flying skills and determination of, 200, 202; grind of the derby, comment about, 182–183; hot-air balloon experiment of, 5; inspiration from and bond between racers after death of Marvel, 187–189, **188**; as inspiration to future pilots, 223; jumping off a building with an umbrella by, 1, 5, 18, 225; lunch before start of race, 105, 108; marriage and family of, 223, 225; marriage of, 42, 63; Marvel's plane, news about from reporter, 133; mechanical trouble, concerns about, 146, 183, 193; memoir of, 221; Mexico trip from El Paso of, 149; newspaper updates writing by, 134, 141, 176, 187, 189, 200, 203; ninth leg flight and finish in Cleveland, 192–196, **195**; placement after derby legs, 117, 131, 146, 152, 158, 162, 168, 170, 173, 178, 181, 192; relationship with father, 19, 172–173; reporter question before start of race, 104; sabotage warning, concern about, 105, 121; second leg flight and finish of, 120, 121, 122, 129, 131; seventh leg flight and finish of, 178, 179, 181; showing off before landing in Columbus, 186–187; sixth leg flight of, 171–173; speeches at banquets, reaction to, 165; speed records of, 223; Speedwing plane assembly and delivery, watching with Marvel, 87–88; telegram to family about win, 200; test flight with Herb, 42; third leg flight and finish of, 137, 140; transport license requirements and flight test of, 63–64; Travel Air crew around plane of during stops, 167; Travel Air job in California of, 19, 40–42; Travel Air visits and aviation job offer with company, 18–19, 171; trophy inscription with Marvel's name and gifting if to parents, 141, 202; weekend with Amelia and Ruth, 203,

274